# THE DEVIL HIMSELF

# Also by Dudley Pope

*NAVAL HISTORY*

*Flag 4*
*The Battle of the River Plate*
*73 North*
*England Expects*
*At 12 Mr Byng Was Shot*
*The Black Ship*
*Guns*
*The Great Gamble*
*Harry Morgan's Way*
*Life in Nelson's Navy*

*NOVELS*

The Ramage Series:
*Ramage*
*Ramage and the Drum Beat*
*Ramage and the Freebooters*
*Governor Ramage R.N.*
*Ramage's Prize*
*Ramage and the Guillotine*
*Ramage's Diamond*
*Ramage's Mutiny*
*Ramage and the Rebels*
*The Ramage Touch*
*Ramage's Signal*
*Ramage and the Renegades*
*Ramage's Devil*
*Ramage's Trial*
*Ramage's Challenge*
*Ramage at Trafalgar*

The Yorke Series:

*Convoy*
*Buccaneer*
*Admiral*
*Decoy*
*Galleon*

# THE DEVIL HIMSELF

## The Mutiny of 1800

BY

*DUDLEY POPE*

*AN ALISON PRESS BOOK*
Secker & Warburg

Distributed by David & Charles, Inc.
North Pomfret, Vermont 05053

First published in England 1987 by
The Alison Press/Martin Secker & Warburg Ltd
54 Poland Street, London W1V 3DF

British Library Cataloguing in Publication Data
Pope, Dudley
The devil himself : the mutiny of 1800.
1. Great Britain. Royal Navy—History
2. Danae (Ship)
3. Mutiny—Great Britain—History
I. Title
359.1'334      VB867.D3

ISBN 0-436-37751-9

Printed by Mackays of Chatham

*For Kay – kindly critic, patient
translator, but never a mutineer!*

# CONTENTS

Author's Preface     xiii

1   Melancholy circumstances     1
2   A voyage to Cayenne     10
3   A prize for the *Indefatigable*     19
4   *Vaillante* to *Danae*     24
5   The Jersey flotilla     36
6   The Channel fleet     47
7   Trials for two captains     60
8   The *Danae*'s last muster     66
9   The organizers     73
10   'The ship's ours now!'     79
11   Surrender at Le Conquet     92
12   The sale of the *Danae*     107
13   Inquest on board the *Gladiator*     114
14   Revolutionary red tape     130
15   The price of mutiny     134
16   The trial of John McDonald     149
17   King George's mercy     159
18   A death in Barbados     169

Notes and Bibliography     177
Index     183

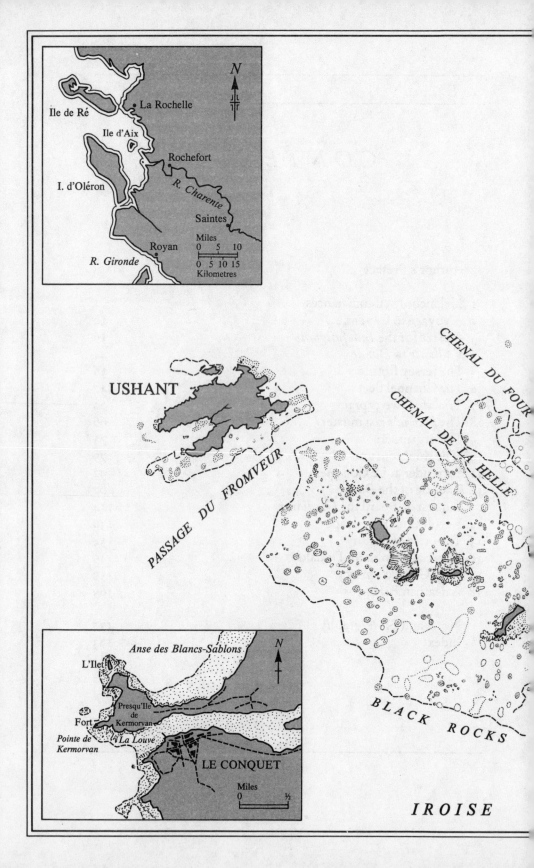

Miles
0    5    10

0  5 10 15
Kilometres

Île de Ré

La Rochelle

Île d'Aix

I. d'Oléron

Rochefort

R. Charente

Saintes

Royan

R. Gironde

USHANT

PASSAGE DU FROMVEUR

CHENAL DU FOUR

CHENAL DE LA HELLE

BLACK ROCKS

IROISE

Anse des Blancs-Sablons

L'Ilet

Presqu'Île
de
Kermorvan

Fort

Pointe de
Kermorvan

La Louve

LE CONQUET

Miles
0              ½

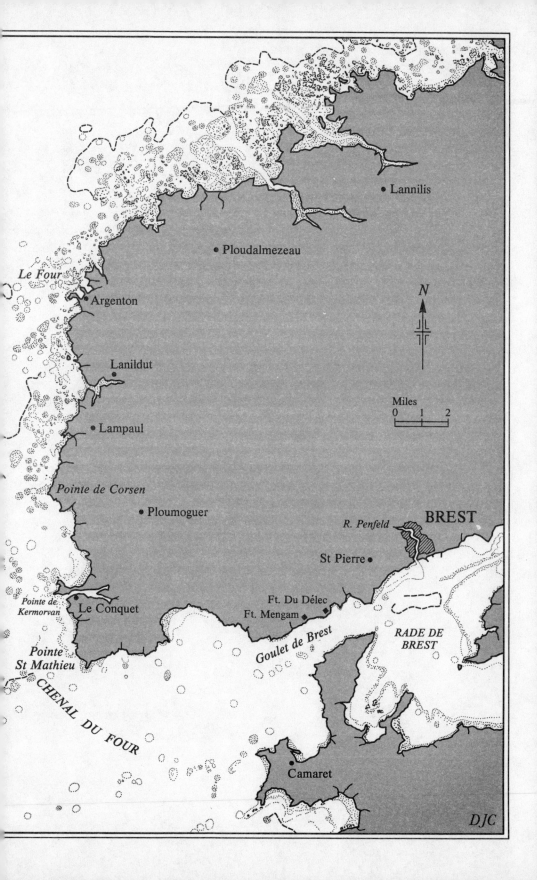

# *AUTHOR'S NOTE*

In the archives at the walled naval headquarters in Brest is a folder labelled *Le Diable Lui-même* (the Devil Himself). It dates from March 1800, and no one knows who gave it that name, but the story emerging from the archives (and those in the Public Record Office in London) is intriguing and poses the question: when was a man an American?

Dudley Pope
French Antilles

# PREFACE

This is the story of a mutiny in the British frigate *Danae* at the turn of the eighteenth century. The reason for the mutiny will never be known for certain, but it is notable because, along with the story of the *Hermione* in the West Indies, it was the only case in a war lasting nearly a quarter of a century of a crew mutinying, seizing a frigate and carrying her into an enemy port (where they were distrusted and meagrely rewarded).

The great mutinies of the Fleet at Spithead and the Nore some years earlier had resulted in improvements of the conditions under which the seamen lived. However, unlike the *Hermione*, which had a sadistically cruel captain whose murder by his crew can raise little sympathy, the mutiny in the *Danae* focuses on two other problems the Navy faced during the whole war: the pressing of men generally, and in particular the pressing of men claiming to be Americans and who held Protections.

The question of Americans and Protections is dealt with in chapter 4. However, it must be remembered that the strength of the Royal Navy during the Revolutionary and Napoleonic wars rested on the press gangs. By 1800 the Royal Navy comprised 110,000 seamen and 20,000 Marines out of a total population of less than nine million. The Navy was in competition with the Army for men, but both were at a disadvantage compared with France, which had universal conscription.

Apart from small parties sent out by individual ships, the press gangs were operated by the Impress Service, which had headquarters in various towns. At the beginning of the war only men connected with the sea were seized, but later any man who appeared to be over eighteen and under fifty-five could be taken. A few classes of men were exempted – for example farm labourers, especially at harvest time, when each was given a certificate showing he was not liable. 'Gentlemen', using their dress as a yardstick, were usually exempted by the gangs, which found that jails and the assizes yielded plenty of men: the justices were only too pleased to give offenders the choice of going to sea or going to jail. However, this did not mean that the press gangs supplied the Navy with hardened criminals: men were sent to jail for a wide variety of offences, many quite minor, and a man brought to court for poaching could find himself at sea serving in a ship of the line within the month.

There was one universal rule: once the man was pressed into the Navy he would serve as long as the war continued. A soldier was in the same position. Many men were freed briefly during the few months of peace following the Treaty of Amiens but were pressed again as soon as the war restarted.

The press gang was of course nothing new. Centuries earlier, before the Royal Navy was established, the Cinque ports had to supply ships and men for the country's defence, and the press was well known to Shakespeare. He has Falstaff, in *Henry IV, Part One*, admitting that he had 'misused the King's press damnably': he had impressed men for the Army and then freed some (especially bachelors about to be married) when bribed. 'I have got, in exchange of a hundred and fifty soldiers, three hundred and odd pounds,' the old villain admitted, saying that he pressed none but 'good householders', but to make up the numbers had to take up 'revolted tapsters and ostlers trade-fall'n; the cankers of a calm world and a long peace . . .'

The treatment of a man after he had volunteered or been pressed into the Navy could be harsh if he misbehaved, although the system was fair inasmuch as every volunteer was paid a bounty of £5, and every pressed man was always given the chance of volunteering when he boarded a ship, so that he received the bounty.

Flogging was common, but it must be remembered that this was a harsh age, and it is absurd to judge it nearly two centuries later by modern humanitarian standards. Lashes were awarded in dozens, a dozen being the usual punishment for drunkenness. A captain was not supposed to award more than two dozen lashes, but when the offence deserved more and the captain could not appeal to higher authority (a process which could take months and involve a court martial) the limit was often ignored. The lash was used universally – the Army flogged miscreants, and the lash was as well known in the French Navy and Army as the British.

More severe punishments such as hanging were rare: all ships at all times were short of men, and the noose was reserved almost entirely for mutiny or treason. Keel-hauling was never performed in the Royal Navy – it is a part of mythology, like pirates making their victims walk the plank (why bother when it was easier to throw the victim over the side?).

The commonest offence in the Royal Navy was drunkenness. The men received a generous ration of spirits each day, and although it was forbidden the real drinkers 'hoarded their tot', keeping their rations until the end of the week, when they had enough to get really drunk. This state was usually ignored unless the man made a nuisance of himself or started fighting. The result then was usually a dozen lashes. The hardened drinkers often reckoned it was worth it: a night supping rum until oblivion made the deck seem soft was reckoned worth a dozen lashes.

In France, a new Republican Calendar was introduced after the Revolution, one with twelve new months of three ten-day weeks. The new months were *Vendémiaire* (part of September and October), *Brumaire* (October–November), *Frimaire* (November–December) and on to *Nivôse, Pluviôse, Ventôse, Germinal* (March–April), *Floréal, Prairial, Messidor, Thermidor* (July–August) and *Fructidor*.

The new Calendar began on 22 September 1792, and the years were dated from then. Thus 1 *Vendémiaire* year two was 22 September 1793, while 10 *Vendémiaire* was 1 October, 11 *Brumaire* the first day of November and 11 *Frimaire* was the first day of December, while 12 *Nivôse* was the first day of January 1794. Year three began on 10 *Vendémiaire* (22 September). By order of the Senate, the old calendar was resumed on 1 January 1806.

As will be seen from the narrative, only three of the *Danae* mutineers were ever captured. There is little doubt that over the years several men (particularly Channel Islanders who spoke fluent French and others claiming to be Americans with Protections) must have changed their names and served in neutral merchant ships or, when captured in French ships, remained undetected by the British and were treated as prisoners of war, being later exchanged or freed when the war ended.

The cause of the mutiny will be discussed as long as men argue about ships and the sea, but it is interesting to compare Lord Proby being so patient with a scoundrel of a carpenter with the captain described to the French by the mutineers; likewise it is difficult to reconcile those descriptions with his behaviour during the last few hours of his life. It is interesting to speculate what would have happened had he not agreed to the request of the master of a transport and taken on board the troublesome seaman McDonald. Was it McDonald's glib tongue that roused up bored and over-worked men into a state of mutiny?

## CHAPTER ONE

# MELANCHOLY CIRCUMSTANCES

Any Briton sitting down to read his copy of *The Times* or *Morning Post* in March 1800 was by then used to the fact that the long war with France had reached a stalemate and that the French conquering armies stretched from the Netherlands to Rome. Admittedly Sir Horatio Nelson had roundly defeated the French fleet at the Battle of the Nile eighteen months earlier, destroying eleven out of thirteen ships of the line, but in the scales of war this victory was balanced against Napoleon's creation of five republics – the Ligurian (Genoa), the Helvetian (Switzerland), Cisalpine (Milan), Roman (the Papal States) and the Parthenopean (Naples).

The recently collapsed coalition of Britain, Austria, Prussia and Russia against the citizen armies of Revolutionary France had anyway seemed a feeble affair to a realist, who was rarely disappointed in his wait for news of defeats and duplicity. Nevertheless, life in London went on quite normally; indeed, although the first two weeks of the month were chilly with showers and a brisk wind, theatres were busy.

*The Times* of 14 March announced the only performance that season of Dryden's *Alexander's Feast*, set to music by Handel. It listed the singers and noted that Mr G. Ashley was 'the leader of the band' while his son, Mr J. Ashley, played the organ. The next day's *Times* gave the usual Court News. The Duke of York, who presided over the Army's affairs at the Horse Guards as Commander-in-Chief, had spent two hours with the King at the Queen's House, and then the King had held a levee at St James's Palace which was 'thinly attended'.

*The Times* also reported that: 'Yesterday was the period fixed on some time since for twenty-four of the largest troopships to be in readiness at Portsmouth. We are informed by a very respectable authority that eighteen thousand men are under orders for immediate service. Admiral Knowles will conduct the naval part of the expedition, of which Sir Charles Stuart will have the command-in-chief.'

The only thing that *The Times* did not reveal was the actual destination of the force, but anyone frequenting the fashionable salons would not have needed telling, because secrecy was almost unknown: gossip spread details almost as soon as they were decided at the Admiralty or Horse Guards. For the French the London newspapers were a good source of intelligence.

However, a few days later the roles of newspapers were reversed, although the intelligence reported in the official French newspaper, *Le Moniteur*, was alarming. On Friday, 28 March, *The Times* in the section headed 'News from France' said:

## MINISTRY OF MARINE

Extract of letter from the *Ordonnateur* of Marine at Brest to the Minister of Marine and Colonies [in Paris] dated March 15th: 'Citizen Minister – a frigate or large English cruiser called the *Danae*, mounting 22 guns of 32 pounders, her crew consisting of 150 men, struck yesterday without firing a shot, in consequence of the movement directed by the intrepid temerity of five French sailors belonging to St Maloes [sic]. She was taken possession of by the corvette *Colombe*, which has conducted her to Conquet. As soon as I shall have received the details of this extraordinary event I shall instantly transmit them to you.
'Note – I have since heard that the *Danae* entered Brest at the same time with the convoy of French ships from the Channel, under the escort of the *Colombe*.'

*The Times* then added:

Telegraphic despatch from Brest of 23rd March. Najac, *Ordonnateur* of Marine at Brest to the Minister of Marine:
'The convoy, the entry of which into the Road [at Brest] has already been announced to you by a telegraphic despatch,

consists of French ships laden with provisions and other stores for the combined naval army. I immediately sent off to Paris the five Frenchmen who prevailed on the crew of the *Danae* to rise, and three Englishmen, in pursuance of your order of 21st March.'

The news item naturally became the main subject of excited conversation and speculation in every London salon and club and, of course, at the Admiralty: mutiny was the most dreadful word in the naval vocabulary. Everyone could remember the bloody mutiny in the *Hermione* off Jamaica less than three years earlier when some of the crew murdered Captain Hugh Pigot and all the commission officers, tossing them overboard before sailing the ship across the Caribbean to a port on the Main and handing her over to the Spanish.

Since then the public had occasionally been reminded of the *Hermione* horror when the Navy caught a mutineer, tried and then hanged him. The fact that Pigot was a sadist had never been made public, but most people knew he had been stabbed to death in his cabin one night and his body thrown out through a window.

Now, according to the *Moniteur*, the *Danae*'s crew had mutinied and handed her over to the French. What had they done to the captain and officers? Surely she was the frigate commanded by the Earl of Carysfort's young son, Lord Proby?

It was an alarming Friday, and everyone waited anxiously for Saturday's edition of *The Times*, which told them:

> Yesterday official advices were received in Town from Plymouth, containing the melancholy circumstances of the capture of the *Danae* frigate, which was mentioned in the Paris papers.
>
> On Wednesday arrived at Plymouth a cartel* from Brest, which brought over the purser, surgeon and captain's clerk of the *Danae*, of 20 guns, Captain Lord Proby, with five other English persons that had been taken prisoners.
>
> It appears that Captain Lord Proby had been cruising on the coast of France, with a squadron under his command, and on the evening of the 14th instant, while most of the officers were

---

* A ship used to carry prisoners being exchanged between Britain and France.

below, a mutiny broke out on board, in which ten Frenchmen appeared to be the ringleaders, headed by an Englishman of the name of Jackson, said to be of Liverpool. The Frenchmen were lately taken [from] on board the *Bordelais*, and permitted to enter into the English service . . . Captain Proby and the Master of the *Danae* are wounded . . . As soon as the mutineers carried their point, they made sail for Brest harbour, and on their arrival were seized by the officers and crews of the ships lying there . . .

The *Lord St Vincent* schooner, of 14 guns, one of the *Danae*'s squadron, returned to Plymouth on Wednesday, not having been able to find her consort, which is accounted for by her having been run away with.

At the time of the mutiny on board the *Danae*, Lord Proby's father was forty-eight years old and serving in Berlin as Britain's Envoy Extraordinary and Minister Plenipotentiary to the court of Prussia – a post to which he had just been appointed.

A man with a slow, tedious voice, he had received the Irish earldom of Carysfort in 1789, when he was a few days short of his thirty-eighth birthday. *The Complete Peerage* noted that he was 'Esteemed a good and elegant scholar. His temper had yet more goodness and elegance to boast of . . .' However, as a public speaker 'his utterance is disagreeably slow, tedious and hesitating, perpetually interrupted by interjections Ah! Ah!'

His first wife, Elizabeth, had been the daughter of an Irish baronet, Sir William Osborne, and they had five children – three sons, of whom the eldest was William, who took the courtesy title of Lord Proby, and two daughters, Charlotte and Elizabeth.

Carysfort married again shortly after his first wife died, and Horace Walpole, in a letter describing a supper he attended, wrote:

We had another pair of lovers, vizt. Lord Carysfort and Miss Grenville, who are rather come to a sober time of life for the amusement of courtship, but they did their best. She is much fallen off, though she never was beautiful.

When Mrs Sheridan and her sister were condescending these words, which they dwelt on a long time, 'This may soothe but cannot cure my pain,' Lord Carysfort fixed his widower's eyes in a most languishing, amorous and significant manner on his love, who did not seem at all at a loss to understand his glances, and whether she was entertained with them or not, there were several of us at the table who were.

Apparently the courtship was genuine because Carysfort, aged thirty-five, married this second Elizabeth, who was a sister of George, the first Marquess of Buckingham, one of the powerful Temple family.

Carysfort decided not to send his eldest son, William Allen, to his old school: instead of Westminster he was sent to Rugby when he was nine years old. Young William had no doubts about the career he wanted to follow: he chose the Navy and joined his first ship as a midshipman when he was fourteen. But the most important aspect of his seagoing career was that one uncle was the Marquis of Buckingham and another was the Marquis's brother, Thomas Temple, while another of the Temple brood was Lord Grenville.

However, life in the midshipmen's berth of a ship of war at this time was hard. It mattered little whether you mustered marquises among your relatives or sheep stealers and higglers: the other midshipmen played cruel tricks, forks were cleaned by digging the prongs into the table cloth (which usually was a large dirty rag) and food was usually little different from that served to the seamen, unless the midshipmen bought extra out of their own pockets. The midshipmen's berth comprised a small cabin furnished with a table and forms, and enough room to sling hammocks and stow the trunks holding their possessions.

Young Proby found that a midshipman's position on board a ship – he was usually one of half a dozen or more – was like that of an officer's apprentice. Seamen old enough to be his grandfather had to call him 'sir' but he had no status among the officers: he was little more than a conveyor of messages and, depending on the captain, still at school, except this was a school where lessons were often learned out on the end of a yard in a gale of wind and where one mistake could mean plunging to a sudden death. A lad picked up knotting and splicing as best he could. If he was lucky, the master taught him the mysteries of navigation and how to use a quadrant and then wrestle with trigonometry to work out a sight, and how 'D.lat over D. Long' (the difference of latitude and the difference of longitude) could, by some mathematical alchemy, equal the distance the ship had run.

Midshipmen were likely to be of any age. They could be curly-haired twelve-year-olds; they could be sturdy and hard-swearing thirty-year-olds who had more than once failed their examination for lieutenant; they could be hard-drinking fifty-year-olds, failed and disillusioned, whose only sport was baiting the youngsters.

Perhaps the most important lessons learned by young midshipmen were the unexpected ones – how to keep awake during the last half an hour of a long night watch, how to tar tarpaulins so that you stayed dry in torrential rain driven by a high wind, and how to keep a good lookout, scanning a horizon from side to side without your eye jumping over a sail which showed up as a tiny speck . . . yes, and how to sleep standing up without the officer of the deck spotting it.

These were all lessons that William Allen, Lord Proby, midshipman, had learned before taking a run at the first professional hurdle he had to face: passing for lieutenant. This meant travelling up to London (the commander-in-chief set up a special board for midshipmen on a foreign station) with certificates from all the captains he had served with, giving the length of time served and a report on his conduct. The certificates had to add up to a total of four years. At the time that Proby took his examination for lieutenant there were ways round the four-year qualification: carrying a young boy's name on the ship's books while he was in fact still at school on shore was one method of getting a year or so's extra service, providing a captain was agreeable, and most were only too glad to help the son of an old friend or placate a dunning tailor.

So Proby passed for lieutenant on 1 March 1796, aged sixteen years and nine months. Soon the Lords Commissioners of the Admiralty would decree that a youth had to be twenty years old before being actually appointed a lieutenant, but this regulation was countered by a youngster taking the examination before he was twenty and (providing he passed) being made lieutenant on his twentieth birthday.

As soon as he was a lieutenant, Proby was sent out to the Mediterranean to serve under Admiral Sir John Jervis (later Lord

St Vincent), who was, with his firm but understanding discipline, the best commander-in-chief for a young officer. However, Sir John had many more officers than ships to command. Fortunately in September 1796 the commanding officer of the 14-gun fireship *Tarleton* was sent back to England (with a letter from Sir John recommending him to the First Lord of the Admiralty, Lord Spencer) and Proby was given command.

She was old and leaky; Proby's ship's company spent much of the time at the pump. In fact in the stiff Mediterranean lop in which she frequently found herself in the Tyrrhenian Sea, she was 'pumped to windward'. But she was a lieutenant's command, and Jervis, who favoured only those officers he reckoned deserved it (a Captain Horatio Nelson among them), no doubt reckoned that if Proby could keep the *Tarleton* afloat he would eventually merit a better command.

The chance came a couple of months later, and Sir John wrote to Lord Spencer: '. . . I have the pleasure to assure you that Lord Proby acquits himself well in his command and I am very happy that he is clear of the *Tarleton*, for she was in extreme danger of going down in the passage from San Fiorenzo to Porto Ferraio [Corsica] . . .'

Proby was even luckier than perhaps he deserved: he had been in his new command, still a lieutenant, when Captain Richard Bowen of the 32-gun frigate *Terpsichore* captured the 34-gun Spanish frigate *Mahonessa* off Cap de Gata. Sir John Jervis, writing to the First Lord from Gibraltar, said: 'The Spanish frigate captured by Captain Bowen in so skilful and officer-like manner, being a beautiful and formidable ship of her class, I have directed Commissioner Inglefield* to cause her to be surveyed, valued and purchased for His Majesty's service; and it is my intention to appoint Captain Giffard to the command of her, to promote Captain Woodhouse to *La Mignonne*, to remove Lord Proby to the *Peterel* . . .'

The capture of *La Mahonessa* was particularly lucky for Proby because in the game of musical chairs among the captains started by her purchase into the Navy, it resulted in him going to a 16-gun

---

* Inventor of the Inglefield clip, well known to signalmen and others who have used it to secure flags to halyards for a century and a half.

sloop. Not only was the *Peterel* a bigger ship than anything he had yet commanded, but she was of a size that rated a 'master and commander' in command. So Lieutenant the Lord Proby, given command of the *Peterel*, automatically became (two days before Christmas in 1796, and aged seventeen and a half) a master and commander. But although he was the captain (i.e. in command) of the *Peterel*, he was not officially a 'captain': he had not been given command of a ship which was rated the command of a post captain.

However, Lord Spencer, who saw Proby's father frequently in Parliament, told Sir John Jervis in a letter: 'I made Lord Carysfort very happy this morning by mentioning to him the good account you give me of Lord Proby. You have established so good a school for young officers that if a lad has anything in him, it must come out.'

The *Peterel*, being only a 16-gun sloop, was one of the smallest in the 'List of King's Ships now in Commission', but she was an essential rung in Proby's climb up the ladder of promotion. In her, he learned the most valuable lesson of all – that command is a lonely business; that the captain of a ship (which he was, even though his rank was 'master and commander') has to remain remote from his officers and ship's company, living and eating in isolation. It was no easy task in a vessel the size of the *Peterel*, which would stand comparison with the Brixham trawler of later years.

He stayed in the *Peterel* in the Mediterranean for fourteen months, when interest obtained him the next vital promotion: he was sent back to the Channel and 'made post', which meant he was 'posted' to command a ship of a size that had to be commanded by a captain. The *Peterel* merited only a 'master and commander', but the 36-gun frigate *Belle Poule*, captured from the French, was a ship of the size to be commanded by a post captain, even if she was simply lying in Plymouth out of commission. Proby was given command of her on 17 February 1798.

Now he was a 'post captain', and from then on his name (and the date that he was 'made post') would be set down in the Navy List, and his seniority would be measured from that date. If he never had another command and remained on half-pay, his name would continue to advance in seniority up the List as those above him died or were killed, and those below him joined in the relentless but slow upward progression. If only he lived long enough, there was nothing to stop Proby becoming an admiral without ever going to sea again; there were cases of officers who had been on the Navy List but unemployed receiving half-pay for many more years than they had served at sea. But a bloody war, natural death or service in somewhere like the West Indies (where yellow fever was by far a worse enemy than roundshot) meant that not too many post captains survived long enough to reach the top of the captains' list, with the automatic spill over to the bottom of the list of admirals, where once again seniority shuffled you upwards.

Proby's appointment to the *Belle Poule* was made solely to get him post rank – and thus on to the post list – at the age of eighteen and a half, and he left the ship after only one month. Although he was unemployed for the next eight months, his name was on the list, piling up seniority – and interest was at work in the Admiralty to get him a new command.

A good deal of nonsense has been written about 'interest'. Yes, Proby was given command of a 36-gun frigate at the age of eighteen and a half, but the ship never went to sea and Proby was on board for only a month. The Admiralty's intention was simply to 'make him post', which could only be done by giving him command (however briefly) of a ship which had to be commanded by a post captain. Without interest it is unlikely that Nelson would ever have commanded a ship, let alone a fleet. There was no question that Proby's next command would be such a big ship; nor was it. On 4 December 1798, just two years after being made 'master and commander' of the *Peterel*, he was given a commission as captain of the *Danae*.

## CHAPTER TWO

# A VOYAGE
# TO CAYENNE

During 1796, while Lord Proby was serving as a lieutenant, French shipwrights, blacksmiths and carpenters were busy working in a shipyard at Bayonne, a quiet and dignified town in the south-western corner of France in the flat, sandy area forming the heart of the Basque country.

The town's main claim to fame (though disputed) was that it gave its name to the bayonet, first made there in the seventeenth century. It was, at the time men were busy in the shipyard, a small town on the River Adour, nestling sleepily at the foot of the Pyrenees which begin only thirteen miles away and rear up to 3,000 feet on the Spanish border.

The shipyard was on the south bank of the river opposite the Citadel, and the town was only three miles from Biarritz on the coast, and ten miles from the Spanish border. For more than one hundred and fifty miles to the north the Atlantic coast is a straight line, edged by sand dunes and backed by flat, sandy land spotted with lakes, several of which are more than a mile long.

The specifications given to the master shipwright at Bayonne were for a corvette designed to carry twenty 8-pounder guns. She was intended to be fast, with fine lines. She would heel easily to begin with and then become progressively stiffer as the wind increased. The 'principal dimensions' marked on her drafts, when they arrived from the Ministry of Marine in Paris, called for an overall length of 113 feet 4 inches, with a beam amidships, outside the frames, of 28 feet 6 inches. When ready for sea, loaded with powder, shot, water and provisions, she should draw 11 feet 1 inch forward and 12 feet 2 inches aft.

She was designed as a flush deck ship: she had no forecastle or poop, and the designers had been ruthless as far as accommodation for the ship's company was concerned: no one could stand upright anywhere below. Perhaps inspired with revolutionary zeal and determined that there should be neither comfort nor privilege for the captain, the captain's cabin had a headroom of 5 feet and was comparable in size to a cramped henhouse.

One of the advantages of building the ship at Bayonne in 1796 was the forests at the foothills of the Pyrenees: there was a plentiful supply of timber, and the British blockade was having little effect yet on shipbuilding. So the workmen, many of them speaking Basque and playing pelota in their spare time, busied themselves with adze and chisel, drill and saw, while the blacksmiths forged the ironwork necessary: gudgeons and pintles for the rudder, hinges for portlids, chainplates for the rigging, and all the hundreds of metal items needed on board a ship. Carpenters' apprentices were given the task of cutting thousands of treenails; planks for the hull had to be cut and shaped; frames needed to be shaped and, where necessary, scarphed in the mould lofts until they matched patterns made out of light wood.

Finally she was completed and launched. Her name was *La Vaillante*, valiant, and once her yards were crossed and sails bent on, she sailed on 25 November 1796 for Rochefort, where she arrived on 2 December for the final fitting out, when her guns were taken from the naval arsenal and swayed on board.

While the fitting out was being completed on board *La Vaillante* and she then waited several months at Rochefort for a captain and ship's company, there was a crisis growing in France's political life. The reasons for this were complex, but as far as it affects this narrative the basic position was that with Prussia and Austria now out of the war, Britain and France faced each other alone. The situation was summed up by H.A.L. Fisher: 'Between them lay two questions, both striking deep into the heart of politics, the Rhine frontier which Britain would never concede, the monarchy which the victorious armies of France would never accept.'

Napoleon was to the south with his Army of Italy, but in Paris the Directory considered itself menaced by royalists, who after the first frenzy of the Revolution were now emerging from hiding or the discreet silence they had found necessary if they were to keep their heads on their shoulders. The pendulum, in other words, was beginning to swing back.

Elections in April 1797 saw only eleven of the two hundred and sixteen former deputies to the Convention elected; most of the new members were monarchists, not republicans. United and properly led (which they were not at the moment), they could be a threat to the Directory. The republican Directors, backed by an emissary sent up to the capital by General Napoleon in Italy, decided to strike against the monarchists.

At dawn on 4 September 1797 (18 Fructidor), Paris found itself occupied by the Army. Carnot, who was the man who had built the Army up to a million men and completely reorganized it until it was the greatest fighting machine ever seen in Europe, promptly fled; Barthélemy, the diplomat who had signed the peace treaty with Prussia after Carnot had planned the victory, did not get away in time, and was arrested.

Hundreds of members of legislative bodies were arrested; elections in nearly fifty departments were cancelled; newspapers and magazines suspected of royalist sympathies were shut down; and by the time the *coup d'état* was over, many priests and dozens of the most important people now regarded by the Directory as enemies of the state had been arrested and, without trial, sentenced to the 'dry guillotine'. This was the name given to banishment to Cayenne, in French Guinea, later to become better known by the name of the nearby Devil's Island, where yellow fever, malaria, blackwater fever and other tropical diseases waited to bring a more lingering death than the one dispensed by the blade of Dr Guillotine's recent invention.

*La Vaillante*, now lying almost completed in Rochefort, needed a captain, and the Ministry of Marine in Paris chose a man of fifty-six, *Lieutenant de vaisseau* Pierre Laporte. Compared with the average age of frigate captains in the Royal Navy – most were in their late twenties or early thirties – Laporte was old for the command of a 20-gun corvette, but the reason was not hard to find.

The first flush of revolutionary zeal meant rooting out (and sending to the guillotine) any royalist – or anyone suspected of having royalist sympathies – from the Navy, Army and both public and private life. In practice this meant that the Navy suffered out of all proportion: most if not all its officers were either royalists or men from aristocratic families the revolutionaries did not trust. The effect was that many captains and admirals were executed or jailed; likewise captains and lieutenants were sacked unless they could convince the new authorities of their revolutionary zest.

However, Revolution or not, ships had to have captains and officers, and the only way of providing enough new ones with any experience was to promote republican warrant and petty officers to commission rank, and turn seamen into warrant officers and petty officers as required. Thus boatswains with the right republican attitude found themselves commanding ships; able seamen became boatswains overnight. Pliant captains became admirals; lineage was sacrificed for promotion.

The effect on the Navy was little short of disastrous. In the Army the idea that every soldier had a field marshal's baton waiting in his knapsack became true in many cases for the simple reason that it is possible to train an Army officer more quickly than a Naval officer: a fact to do with the sea and its varied nature, not with any intellectual difference between a land and sea officer.

In many cases, where former experienced warrant and petty officers had been made lieutenants or given command of ships, this meant that the average age of captains tended to be high, and this mattered in the case of smaller ships like corvettes and frigates because ideally they needed younger men who could provide the necessary dash and better stand up to the discomfort and hardship. In the case of *La Vaillante* it was hard for a fifty-six-year-old man to spend much of his day in quarters with 5 feet headroom: bones and muscles nearly sixty years old would creak and protest, where a twenty- or thirty-year-old might dismiss it all as a nuisance.

As soon as Lieutenant Laporte had arrived on board *La Vaillante*, mustered a ship's company and provisioned and watered his ship, he received orders to prepare to embark a number of *déportés* and take them across the Atlantic to exile in Cayenne. With her low headroom and lack of space below, *La Vaillante* was far from a suitable vessel for carrying *déportés*, but she was just built, with the bottom newly coppered, and neither the Directory nor the Ministry of Marine and the Colonies was prepared to use a bigger ship. Apart from anything else, the British were patrolling the whole French Atlantic coast, trying to enforce a blockade, and a small fast ship stood a better chance of getting away.

The *déportés*, all victims of the *coup d'état* of 18 Fructidor, were first imprisoned on the Ile d'Aix, a tiny, half-moon-shaped island no more than two miles long, almost completely surrounded by rocks and less than five miles off the mouth of the Charente, the river on which Rochefort stands. The carpenters at Rochefort built a bulkhead in *La Vaillante* below deck, separating the *déportés'* quarters from those of the ship's company. This work was completed by early September and *La Vaillante* dropped down the river and then sailed over to anchor off the Île d'Aix on 21 September.

Laporte had been given the names of the *déportés*, and one of the most striking among the famous was the second on the list, François Barthélemy – the diplomat who had signed the peace treaty with Prussia on behalf of France. Now, sentenced to the 'dry guillotine' and separated from his family, the Directory had allowed Barthélemy only one luxury: alone among the other *déportés*, Barthélemy was being allowed to take a servant with him, Mazarin Le Tellier being prepared to share his master's banishment.

One of the other famous names on the list of *déportés* was that of Charles Pichegru, the general who had conquered the Netherlands. General Pichegru was one of the young generals who, along with men like Masséna, Jourdan and Bonaparte, had made France's new revolutionary armies the masters of Europe. Now, along with Barthélemy the diplomat, Pichegru was about to be sentenced by his former colleagues to end his days in Cayenne (although he later escaped back to France, where he died in mysterious circumstances in 1804).

Other names on the list told a story of aristocrats who had at first joined the Revolution and then drawn back a pace or two, enough to provoke the *coup d'état* of 18 Fructidor – men with names like Charles Honorine Bethelet de la Villeheurnois and Joseph Stanislaus Rovers. Unknown to Rovers at the time, his wife Marie Justine, his three-year-old son Adolphe, and the boy's governess, Sophie Haude, were to be sent out later in *La Vaillante* to join him in his banishment to Cayenne, although, as this narrative will show, it is unlikely that he ever saw them again.

*La Vaillante*'s boats brought the *déportés* on board on 23 September, and soon after boats from Rochefort brought out more things sent out by their families, many of whom had come down to Rochefort. The *Commandant des Armes* gave his permission for money, bills of exchange, clothing, provisions and other items to be sent out to them. The *déportés* had been on board only two days when a sudden squall made *La Vaillante* drag her anchor, so that she drifted towards the shallows of the Baie d'Yves, but Laporte was able to get the anchor up and the ship under way again, to re-anchor in Aix Roads. The next day the ship sailed for Cayenne.

Once clear of the Pointe de Chassiron, at the north end of the Île d'Oléron, Laporte steered to the south-west, first to pick up the northerlies he could expect off the Portuguese coast, and then gradually to work his way into the north-east trades, which would carry him across the Atlantic to French Guinea, on the South American coast next to Brazil, just north of the mouth of the Amazon and the Equator. *La Vaillante* was just three weeks out of Rochefort when lookouts sighted a sail, and Laporte guessed she must be British, bound for one of the Windward or Leeward Islands. He soon overhauled her and sent across a boarding party, who found she was called the *Miss Polly* (noted in *La Vaillante*'s log as the 'Messpoly') with ten men on board. Laporte took them off and they were imprisoned among the *déportés*, while he put a prize crew on board her with orders to make for Cayenne.

Thomas Forster, the master of the *Miss Polly*, was particularly unlucky that *La Vaillante*'s destination was Cayenne, although both his crew and the *déportés* were lucky inasmuch as *Miss Polly* carried a surgeon. It is not clear from the French records whether this man, Thomas Matthews, was a member of the ship's company or a passenger. (It is unlikely that such a small ship would have been carrying a surgeon as part of the crew.)

Cayenne is a small town on an island formed by two rivers. It was then not much more than a humid swamp five degrees north of the Equator, with mosquitoes swarming from the mangroves. The sun made metal too hot to touch: drinking water was simply rainwater – always in plentiful supply, torrential much of the time, and caught in butts. A few miles north along the coast were three islands, the largest of which would soon become a penal colony known throughout the world as Devil's Island, but for the moment *déportés* were landed at Sinnamary, a village on Cayenne, from which there was no escape; the only way out was death which, because of the tropical diseases, was a constant visitor.

The *déportés* had to put up with the crowded quarters in *La Vaillante* for six weeks, eating the same salt tack as the crew, but on reduced rations because they were rated as 'supernumeraries' for victualling. The corvette arrived at Cayenne on 11 November 1797.

Laporte was delighted with the performance of his ship, but he was less than happy about two of his officers; in fact he discharged one of them, *Enseigne de vaisseau* Dubois, on 18 January and *Enseigne de vaisseau* Rivière on 25 January. When *La Vaillante* sailed from Cayenne, bound for Rochefort, she was short of two officers. On the way back Laporte was again lucky to find a prize, which he sent on to Rochefort: this time the British ship (noted in *La Vaillante*'s log as the *Hope*) had only seven men on board, including the master, Gordon Richardson, and they were taken on board the corvette while a prize crew was sent over to sail the *Hope*.

Laporte, once he had arrived back in Rochefort, was so pleased with *La Vaillante*'s performance and the speed of his double crossing of the Atlantic that he wrote a special report. This began by listing where the corvette had been built and how she was armed, along with her main dimensions. He then (with obvious pride) described her sailing qualities. She steered very easily and carried the wind well, his report said, but she heeled noticeably until she gained her best speed. Although her rolling was very lively, her pitching in a sea was very easy. She went to windward at nine and a half knots but with the wind on the beam and all plain sail set to the topgallants, she made twelve knots. With the wind aft her performance was 'very ordinary'. In general, Laporte wrote, the ship was very lively in a good breeze and needed a small amount of weather helm when close hauled. She tacked very well and with the wind aft she wore well, both tacking and wearing being 'very prompt'.

Comparing her speed with other ships, Laporte said proudly, she had always caught up with any vessel she had sighted ahead of her. As far as trim was concerned, she sailed best with the ballast well aft. She needed the masts raked aft and the preventers slack, he added. The work remaining to do in the ship was to knock down the bulkhead 'which had been erected to separate the *déportés*'. He did not realize that there were still many people in jail waiting to be shipped to Cayenne.

Laporte went on a short leave and then returned to the ship, which remained at anchor in the Charente River. Spring came to Brittany and summer had arrived before the *Commandant des Armes* at the port of Rochefort was writing to the Minister of Marine in Paris on 3 August 1798: 'I have the honour to inform you that the corvette *La Bayonnaise* on the 15th of this month embarked 120 individuals condemned to deportation to Cayenne. The corvette *La Vaillante* has received orders to return to the Île de Ré where she must embark 52 passengers also condemned to deportation.'

The orders Laporte finally received told him to take five *déportés* on board from the jail in Rochefort and forty-five more from the Île de Ré. There were in fact fifty *déportés* and three wives. It was not easy for a wife to accompany her husband into exile. Joseph Marie Avine, who had been arrested at his home in Lille very soon after his wedding and sentenced to deportation, had appealed to the Minister of Marine, so against his name it was noted that 'This man is married and in view of the permission granted by the Minister of Marine on 9 Messidor in the year 6, Guillette Le Forestier, his wife, could also embark with him.'

Pierre Claude Buignet was equally fortunate: the Minister had given permission for his wife, Françoise-Catherine Thomate Guillemmette (listed, as is the French custom, under her maiden name), to go into exile with him. She had travelled to Rochefort from their home in Amiens.

The bravery of women 'authorized to follow their husbands' cannot be overestimated: one woman was giving up her life in Lille, the other in Amiens, to be with their husbands in what was, at that time, the most dreadful known place: not for nothing was Cayenne known as the 'dry guillotine': those sent there would almost certainly die of sickness, and they would be no less dead than if they had been strapped down on to the ordinary guillotine.

The third woman sailing to join her husband in Cayenne was Marie Justine Angélique Belmont Rovers, who had her young son Adolphe with her, and Mlle Sophie Haude, the boy's governess.

Mme Rovers' husband had, of course, been taken to Cayenne in *La Vaillante* on the ship's maiden voyage. The Rovers' entourage were regarded as *passagers libres* so presumably were not subject to the same discipline as the *déportés*. There were also two surgeons, Martin and Delivet, being taken out 'at the expense of the government'.

Against the names of the *déportés* waiting on the Île de Ré were listed the towns and departments whence they came, and the list just about covered all of France, ranging from Marie Lavaux, from nearby Lorient, to François Pelletier, who was from St Omer, in the Pas de Calais; from Benoît Robin of Toulon to Jean François Damoiseau of Besançon; from François Alexandre Gros of Paris to Pierre Bourgeois of Valenciennes, where there was the great prison for British prisoners of war.

Laporte now had his full complement of officers: Louis Bequier was the master (mate under the French system), Arnaud Bouchardeau was one *enseigne de vaisseau* and Jean la Peyrère the other, while this time *La Vaillante* carried a surgeon's mate, although among the passengers were, of course, the two surgeons travelling out to Cayenne. There were also several priests among the *déportés*; unfortunately the list does not distinguish them.

So *La Vaillante* sailed up to the Île de Ré after taking on board the five in the jail at Rochefort, and the rest of the *déportés*, including a wide-eyed young Adolphe Rovers, were brought out in the ship's boats and herded below to the section forward closed off by a bulkhead, which had not been removed after *La Vaillante*'s first voyage to Cayenne.

The *Commandant des Armes* at Rochefort wrote to the Minister of Marine on 12 August to report: 'I have the honour to acquaint you of the departure of the corvette *La Vaillante* on 6th August 1798 bound for Cayenne carrying 52 individuals condemned to deportation. The corvette *Bayonnaise*, bound on the same mission, left on the 8th August.'

## CHAPTER THREE

# A PRIZE FOR THE INDEFATIGABLE

*I*n August 1798, the 44-gun British frigate *Indefatigable*, commanded by Captain Sir Edward Pellew, was cruising along the French coast between Ushant and the Spanish border.

Now forty-one years old, Sir Edward was one of the most famous and successful frigate captains in the Royal Navy. He and his brother Israel (who would end his career as Vice Admiral Sir Israel Pellew, while Edward would become Admiral Lord Exmouth) were the sons of the former commander of one of the Dover packets. Edward had served in the American War as a young lieutenant, and was commanding the frigate *Nymphe*, 36 guns, at the beginning of the war with France. Almost as soon as the war began, he met the 40-gun French frigate *Cleopatra*, and captured her – the first of war and an episode which won him a knighthood.

From 1794 onwards he spent most of the time commanding a small squadron in the area off Brest. On 21 September that year he captured the 44-gun frigate *Révolutionnaire* (taken into the British service under the same name, and due to appear again later in this narrative), and Pellew ended the year having captured a total of nine ships. With almost monotonous regularity he sent his captures into Plymouth with prize crews on board, and the prizes he took were a generous mixture of French national ships and privateers. He was made a baronet in 1796, and started off the next year fighting one of the bravest frigate actions recorded.

The *Indefatigable* was in company with the 36-gun frigate *Amazon* on 13 January when Pellew sighted the 74-gun French ship of the line *Les Droits de l'Homme* close to the Penmarchs, making for Brest. It was blowing a gale with heavy seas. For sixteen and a half hours the two British frigates chased the French ship and much of the time the men at the frigates' guns were up to their waists in water. Heavy seas broke over the ships so often that the gunners, having just loaded, frequently saw a sea hit the muzzle of their gun, pouring salt water down on to the charge, soaking the powder. This meant getting out the shot and then, using a wormer – a long pole with a spiral hook on the end like a corkscrew – drawing out the sodden bag of gunpowder and sliding in a fresh charge.

In moonlight towards the end of the action, after darkness fell, Pellew knew that there was a good chance of all three ships ending up on the rocks. His men were worn out and the ship had four feet of water in her hold, water which had flooded in at the ports and sluiced below. The frigate had been rolling so violently during the chase that some of the guns had broken their breechings four times while others had pulled out the ring bolts to which the breechings were made fast.

The French ship (which had been making for Ushant after an expedition to Ireland) had 1,300 men on board. Of these about one hundred sailors and soldiers had been killed in the battle and one hundred and fifty wounded. Just as land was sighted in the moonlight by both the *Indefatigable* and the French ship, the *Droits de l'Homme* lost her foremast and bowsprit. She tried to anchor but this anchor (the only one left: the others had been lost in Bantry Bay, Ireland) dragged, and slowly the ship drove ashore in Audierne Bay. While the *Amazon* drove on shore a couple or miles away, the *Indefatigable* managed to fight her way off the Penmarchs in enormous seas.

That was how Pellew began the year, and then he captured a series of privateers – including the brig *La Basque* on 30 April and *La Nouvelle Eugénie*, of 16 guns, on 11 May. But then he took a swing to the south, to the Canary Islands, capturing the corvette *Ranger* near Tenerife on 14 October. He was unlucky with this ship because she was retaken by the French but captured again by the *Galatea* on 6 November. In the meantime, on 25 October, Pellew had captured the privateer *La Hyène*, armed with 20 guns and with 230 men on board. He found out that his latest capture had once been British – the *Hyena*, captured by the French in 1794.

Returning north again, Pellew started off 1798 by taking the 12-gun *Le Vengeur* in the Channel on 4 January, followed by the

8-gun *L'Inconcevable* on 16 January and *L'Heureuse Nouvelle*, of 22 guns, on 28 January.

Soon after dawn broke on 7 August 1798, when the *Indefatigable* was off the mouth of the River Gironde and the lookouts could 'see a grey goose at a mile', they had been sent aloft and had reported a sail in sight ahead. The ship was obviously steering south-west, planning to round the north-western tip of Portugal. It was obvious to Pellew that the vessel must have come from one of the French ports like Brest or Rochefort to be in this position and on this course.

Immediately the *Indefatigable* started to chase, but the ship ahead was hull-down on the horizon and the wind was light. At a distance of more than a dozen miles, all that could be made out from the *Indefatigable*'s mastheads was that she had three masts, and it was soon apparent that she had sighted the *Indefatigable* and was doing her best to escape. Which meant, of course, that the ship was indeed French.

She was in fact *La Vaillante*, with all the *déportés* on board. She had sailed from Aix Roads on 6 August in good weather but light winds, and once clear of the entrance to the bight had turned south along the coast, keeping in close for the first hundred miles to avoid any blockading British ships. When abreast the mouth of the Gironde she had turned south-west to round Spanish Finisterre and, with any luck, pick up the Portuguese trade winds which would sweep her south-west down towards the Canary Islands, ready to begin the westward Atlantic crossing.

That was Lieutenant Laporte's intention. The first few hours of any passage were always difficult, especially for a small ship like *La Vaillante*, carrying many more people than she was designed for. Among the *déportés* there were the usual percentage of people being seasick, and *La Vaillante*'s own ship's company, many of whom had not been to sea before (several of the gunners had been drafted from artillery regiments of the Army), were still settling down to the sea routine.

A fifty-year-old seaman, Jean Perrier, giving evidence more than a year later at the routine court martial of Laporte, told the court that at 6 o'clock in the morning on 7 August, 'I knew of a warship lying astern of *La Vaillante* at about fourteen miles distant . . .'

Very soon Laporte realized that although the wind was light the enemy ship was gaining on him. *La Vaillante* was heavily laden with the *déportés* and the extra provisions and water needed for them, and Laporte decided that if he was going to escape he was going to have to lighten the ship. The ship's boat was hoisted out and dropped into the sea, and seamen then went to work on the ship's galley. Heavy firebricks stopped the fire from heating the wood of the deck, and the big coppers – in which all food was boiled – were bulky. So all the firebricks and the coppers were thrown over the side.

While this was going on, seamen were sent aloft with buckets on long lines, so that they could hoist up water and throw it over the sails to wet them, this old trick being based on the idea that the water stopped any wind escaping through the weave of the sails. The sails were large and the effect of the buckets small because they inevitably swung into a shroud or yard and spilled some of the water.

Laporte was still concerned about weight: having 'demolished the oven and thrown the pieces over the side', Perrier said, they 'threw two anchors over the side ... and did all possible to increase the speed of the ship'.

Another member of *La Vaillante*'s crew, François Huguenin, who was a thirty-five-year-old corporal of the 5th brigade of Marine Artillery and was embarked in *La Vaillante* as the second master gunner, said that by 9 o'clock the pursuer was getting nearer and the course they were steering, west-south-west, was seen 'to be an advantage to the pursuer'. Laporte altered course to the south, 'under all sails and studding sails'. He was risking being trapped: steering south was the fastest course, but he would soon be caught against the Spanish coast. Yet steering south-west, to avoid the trap, gave the advantage to the enemy.

At nightfall, according to Perrier, 'the warship was not more than two leagues from us and the captain ordered us to general quarters. All night the wind was very weak.'

Huguenin was more definite: 'At nightfall the warship was in our wake.'

At 2 o'clock in the morning 'the warship was within range,' Perrier said, 'and maintained this distance. At 4 o'clock the English warship confirmed his identity by hoisting the English flag and firing two broadsides, which did us much damage.' According to

Huguenin, one of the *Indefatigable*'s shot cut the mizen boom toppinglift, sending the boom crashing down on to the heads of the officers and men on the corvette's quarterdeck.

Pellew, knowing that he had the faster ship (with more than double the number of guns), stayed on *La Vaillante*'s starboard quarter, occasionally turning away to rake the corvette with his broadside guns, as though rattling the bars. Laporte knew that his 8-pounders could do little harm but those on the starboard quarter were trained round as far aft as possible.

'The captain then raised the national flag and ordered our guns to open fire,' Perrier said. 'After a little time the enemy fired several broadsides, to which we replied. But the enemy was too strong for us to continue the fight which, without doubt, decided the captain to lower the flag at 5 o'clock in the morning.'

When Sir Edward Pellew sent over a boarding party to take possession of his latest prize, the young lieutenant was startled to find that she had on board four women, several priests and a small boy, all of whom were terrified by the gunfire. After questioning, Pellew was surprised to find that he had not only captured an almost new French corvette but had rescued half a hundred *déportés* who had, until then, expected to end their days in the swamps of Cayenne.

Pellew, a staunch Protestant, is said to have used the opportunity, when selecting a prize crew to take *La Vaillante* into Plymouth, of getting rid of some of the wilder Irish Catholics among his crew and they, finding themselves among so many priests, were soon asking for, and receiving, blessings.

Within a few hours, with *La Vaillante*'s officers and ship's company on board the *Indefatigable* as prisoners and the prize crew laying a course for Plymouth, probably the most distraught person was Mme Rovers: instead of joining her husband in Cayenne she was now a prisoner of the British, and who knew when (or indeed if) young Adolphe would see his father again. . .?

For more than fifty *déportés*, however, Sir Edward Pellew had wrought a miraculous rescue. Instead of the jungles of Cayenne, they would live in the English countryside. (The priests ended up in a monastery in Dorset where, Pellew's biographer records, they prayed for him daily, and 'to so staunch a Protestant this would have been a source of alarm. He did not, however, hear of it until long afterwards.')

## CHAPTER FOUR

# VAILLANTE TO DANAE

Some of the Royal Navy's best ships had French or Spanish names – they were prizes and the British rarely changed the names when they captured them: indeed when Pellew took the French frigate *La Révolutionnaire*, which had what might have been considered by their Lordships at the Admiralty an unsuitable name to be on the list of the Royal Navy, it was not changed and few seemed aware of the irony of 'His Majesty's frigate *La Révolutionnaire*'.

*La Vaillante* was sailed into Plymouth with a red ensign over the Tricolour, and the *déportés* were landed. There is no mention of what became of the criminals among them but the priests, as mentioned earlier, went off to the monastery nearby. Unfortunately there is also no record of what happened to Mme Rovers, her son or the governess. They certainly never reached Cayenne (although they may have returned to France during the short peace following the Treaty of Amiens).

The corvette was surveyed by the master shipwright at Plymouth, John Marshall, and the master mastmaker, Thomas Jenner, and the commander-in-chief decided to 'buy her in'. This meant that the corvette's hull, masts, spars, rigging and everything else on board her, down to sand glasses and pots and pans, were valued, and the price the Navy paid was based on this. The money then went into the prize account of Pellew, his officers and the ship's company of the *Indefatigable*, every man receiving a percentage according to his rank in the ship.

Once *La Vaillante* was bought into the Navy her name was changed (as if in defiance of the tradition that the name was kept unless wildly inappropriate, but perhaps because there was already a *Valiant*) and the ship was given the new name of *Danae*, the daughter of Acrisius, the King of Argos. The mythical Danaë had a turbulent life which compares with the future of her namesake. The French and Spanish designed beautiful ships. Their designers had achieved that happy blend of art and science which eluded British constructors. Unfortunately for the *Danae*, the 20-gun corvette, flush decked, was a type of ship not built for the Royal Navy. So when the Navy Board considered her future, they ignored her fine lines (which meant that extra weight would make her float so excessively low that her performance would be ruined) and considered her armament.

When captured, she carried twenty 8-pounder guns. British 8-pounders weighed (depending on the length of the barrel) between 17 and 23 hundredweight. We can take the lower figure, so the weight of the *Danae*'s guns, as armed by the French, was 17 tons. These French guns were removed but were not replaced by British 8-pounders; instead the ship was fitted with twenty heavy, stubby-barrelled 32-pounder carronades, which weighed 17 hundredweight each, and twelve 12-pounder carronades, each weighing $5\frac{1}{4}$ hundredweight.

This meant that (with two 'long sixes', the famous 6-pounders, weighing 12 hundredweight each and which were also fitted on the maindeck) the *Danae* was now carrying more than 21 tons, with all the weight high up in the ship: tophamper as high in the hull as it could be fitted, since the carronades were mounted on the maindeck. But even worse, in the *Danae*'s shot locker were not 8-pounder roundshot but 32-, 12- and 6-pounders. Likewise grape and canister shot were also increased, so the *Danae* was laden with about ten more tons.

The effect on the fine-lined *Danae* was like using a racehorse in a dungcart. What Laporte had already reported as a tender ship – after his return from the first voyage to Cayenne he had said that the ship (although fast) heeled until she had picked up speed, but was 'very lively' when rolling – now had the weight of her guns increased by more than half, the extra weight being put in the worst possible place, high up in the ship.

William James, the best historian of this war at sea, wrote of the *Danae*: 'Here is a forcible illustration of the way in which the British usually equip French ships of war, particularly corvettes:

they give them more guns and fewer men, than they were ever intended to carry.* If, when thus burdened with tophamper the ship sails badly or upsets, the fault is laid to the manner of her construction, and a general anathema is pronounced on "French corvettes".' He names six other well-known prizes, former French ships, and asks: 'What can be alleged against such "flush-decked corvettes" . . . ?'

Various other alterations were made in the ship, including cutting some scuttles (portholes) forward. These, as Laporte noted in his report on the ship, had not been fitted when the ship was built. The masts and spars were not changed, but she was given British sails because the Royal Navy very sensibly standardized the dimensions.

The *Danae* had been handed over to the dockyard in late September 1798, by which time all the paperwork had been completed for buying her in and the Navy Board had decided on the disastrous changes to be made. The French guns and their carriages were hoisted out and the shipwrights went to work fitting the slides for the carronades. Ordinary guns were fitted to carriages which had four wheels (trucks) and when each gun was fired it recoiled on the wheels, restrained by a heavy rope (the breeching) secured to the side of the ship and which fitted through either a ring or a protrusion on the breech of the gun itself.

Carronades, apart from the earlier models, operated on slides. The slide was secured on the deck and the whole carronade was fitted in to a sloping platform which ran back in the slide when the carronade fired. The whole slide was pivoted at its forward (outboard) end so that it could be trained round. The slides were as heavy as carriages, but their advantage was that because of the slope outboard the carronade, usually heavier than a gun, could be loaded and run out more easily and quickly and, with the limited recoil – the gun was driven uphill – the slide took up less room than a carriage.

But slides had to be fitted by shipwrights, whereas a gun and carriage could be swayed on board and, once the breeching was

---

* The French later refused to have the *Danae* back for naval service, declaring that she would no longer sail properly. While serving with the Royal Navy her captain, as this narrative later describes, was perpetually bedevilled by a shortage of seamen.

rove through the ringbolt in the ship's side, was ready to fire. The 32-pounder carronades used the same gunports as the original French guns, but new ports had to be cut forward and aft for the extra 12-pounders and the two long sixes (which were on carriages).

Alterations had to be made in the shot locker. While she sailed under the French flag, the ship used only one size of shot, 8-pounders. Now she needed roundshot for the 32-pounder carronades (6.25 inches in diameter), the 12-pounder carronades (4.52 inches) and the long 6-pounders (3.67 inches), quite apart from grape and case shot.

The *Danae* had long since received the first of her ship's company. The names of four Irishmen started off the *Danae*'s new muster roll and all four were pressed men, sent from the *Thisbe*. No captain ordered to send some of his men to another ship could resist the opportunity of getting rid of the worst, so even though they were rated able seamen it is unlikely that men like John Murphy, put down as from Kinsale and twenty-six years old, were very keen on joining a new ship with no headroom and no cook – indeed, a dead ship in the dockyard, secured alongside a hulk. The other three men, also listed as from Kinsale, were James Brown, thirty-five, David Murphy, twenty-four, and Cornelius Shehan (so spelled in the muster roll).

However, Shehan did not stay long: he took advantage of the disorganized state of the *Danae* in the dockyard to desert nine days later. There are only three ways of recording in a muster roll the departure of a man from the King's service: in the appropriate column is noted 'D', for discharged (to another ship or to the hospital), 'D.D.' for discharged dead, or 'R', for run. Thus against Shehan's name in the *Danae*'s first muster roll is noted 'R 29 September 1798 at Plymouth'.

From then on a steady trickle of men were sent to the *Danae*. On 12 October a Lancashire man, Joseph Dobson, nineteen years old and from Warmington, was sent on board and noted down as pressed and a landsman. A few days late a Bristol man, Thomas Jarvis, an able seaman, was sent over from the *Magnificent*.

Finally, on 17 November, the *Danae* received seventeen men to form something of a nucleus of a ship's company, and their origins tell the story of how Britain manned its Navy at this time. In the

order in which they are noted down in the muster roll, Thomas
Thorne, an able seaman, was twenty-five years old and from Poole,
Dorset – a man who had grown up within sight and sound of the
sea. Thomas Grantham, twenty-seven years old and one of the
carpenter's crew, came from London and was a volunteer. Francis
Flintiff, twenty-six years old and from Whitby, was a quartermaster and probably learned his seamanship on board merchant ships
plying from his home town.

The next man was a volunteer from Antrim, in Ireland: James
Gilliland, twenty-eight years old, an able seaman and a name to
remember. The next man was a Londoner, a thirty-seven-year-old
seaman named Thomas Vickers, while the sixth man came from
Rotherham, in Yorkshire: thirty-nine-year-old John Hall, who
was yeoman of sheets.

The ship's corporal was a Scot, forty-one-year-old James
Sheriff, from Aberdeen. William Moore, quartermaster's mate,
was a volunteer from London while the next in the roll, John
Huxley, who was transferred from the *Cambridge*, was a thirty-
one-year-old able seaman from Flint.

The next three men, all in their twenties, came from Hull, Bristol
and Belfast. The next two both came from Cornwall. The last three
in the draft came from Ireland, Maldon (Essex, and written by the
clerk filling in the roll as 'Moulden') and Newfoundland.

Getting the warrant and commission officers was a slow job: the
demand for skilled men like carpenters and boatswains was great.
One of the first warrant officers sent to the *Danae*, in view of the
considerable alterations that were being made to her to accommodate the extra guns, was William Johnson, the carpenter. But he
could not resist the opportunity afforded by being in a ship in the
dockyard with no officers, and on 14 December, before he had
been on board three weeks, he deserted, and six days later John
Chubb was appointed in his place. Chubb, as will be seen later, was
another 'King's bad bargain'.

The Secretary of the Board of Admiralty began sending out
letters which would mean that coaches to Plymouth would soon be
carrying officers for the *Danae*. On 4 December, Lord Proby
received his commission as captain – a good command, since she
was a new ship just completing a refit. Proby's first task, once he
received his commission, was to board the ship – now rated a

frigate – and assemble the officers and ship's company. He would then read aloud to them his commission – thus 'reading himself in' and establishing himself as the lawful captain of the ship.

On the day after he sent off Lord Proby's commission, the Secretary sent out the commissions for the lieutenants. The first was to Charles Niven, who would be the ship's first lieutenant. The second was for Corbett Gosselin, whose commission was also dated 5 December. However, for a reason which is not now clear, but probably because he did not get on with Lord Proby, Gosselin left the ship on 21 January, to be replaced as second lieutenant by the Hon. James Rollo.

Niven and Gosselin completed the commission officers appointed to the *Danae*, but there were several warrant officers yet to come. (The difference between a commission and a warrant officer is that one is appointed by the commission from the King and the other by a warrant from one of the Boards.) Proby was fortunate that among the early warrant officers sent to the ship was John Hollowood as boatswain, and he was followed a month later by Israel Lewis as gunner and then Thomas Mills as purser.

The most important man in a ship of war after the captain is the first lieutenant, and Proby was fortunate that Charles Niven was a competent and experienced officer. He had passed for lieutenant in 1796, his name being almost exactly in the middle of the more than two hundred men who passed for lieutenant in that year. He served first in the *Tysyphone* sloop and spent most of the next year on board the transport *L'Espion*, at Woolwich, before going to the 18-gun brig *Jalouse* for a few months' service in the North Sea. On New Year's Eve 1797, he went to the *Busy*, another 18-gun brig serving in the North Sea, before being sent to the *Ethalion* in April to replace a lieutenant taken ill. This brought him from the North Sea to Plymouth, because the *Ethalion*, a 38-gun frigate, was refitting there.

The *Danae*'s surgeon, Thomas Hendry, whose warrant was dated 14 December, was a complete newcomer to ships and the sea: the *Danae* was his first ship after being accepted into the Navy as a surgeon on production of his certificates from the Surgeon's Hall in Lincoln's Inn Fields and the Sick and Hurt Board.

Just before Lord Proby arrived on board, the *Danae* received another draft of eight men, as cosmopolitan a collection as he was ever to find. One of the first men to join the ship had been the captain's clerk, Samuel Giles, twenty years old, from nearby Kingsand, in Devon. It was his job to fill in the details of every man in the muster roll, and like most clerks serving in the King's ships, he had to write the best approximation he could to a foreigner's name. Thus, although he was not strictly speaking a foreigner, the first man in the new draft was listed as twenty-two years old, from Derry, and under 'Name' Giles wrote 'Johro Sylva (alias de Sylvaz)'. The next was John Knap, twenty-three years old and an able seaman from 'America'. Third in the draft was a thirty-five-year-old gunner's mate from Dublin, Barnett McGuire, while the next was the second man in the ship from Whitby, an able seaman named James Cochrane, who was forty-five. Both McGuire and Cochrane were names to remember. Then came another Irishman, Jeremiah Donovan, a forty-year-old seaman sent over from the *Blenheim*.

The next man represented the Border country, John Elliot, an able seaman from Berwick, while Roger Mills, the coxswain, was thirty-three years old and the third man from Whitby. The last in the draft was a Welshman, James Watts, who was entered as quartermaster's mate.

Lord Proby went on board the ship after coming down from London in a postchaise and, assembling everyone aft, read himself in. The commission was a lengthy document and began with the time-honoured 'By the Commissioners for Executing the Office of Lord High Admiral of the United Kingdom of Great Britain and Ireland, etc'.

It went on:

By virtue of the power and authority to us given, we do hereby constitute and appoint you captain of His Majesty's ship the *Danae* willing and requiring you forthwith to go on board and take upon you the charge and command of her accordingly: strictly charging and commanding all the officers and company of the said ship to behave themselves jointly and severally in their respective employments, with all due respect and obedience unto you their said captain . . .

The commission ended with a stern warning: 'Hereof nor you nor any of you may fail as you will answer to the contrary at your peril; and for so doing this shall be your warrant . . .' It was signed by Evan Nepean, Secretary to the Board, and three members – Lord Arden and Vice Admirals James Gambier and Robert Man.

Having read himself in, Lord Proby had the wearisome task of turning the *Danae* back into a ship of war after so many weeks of being little more than a hulk in the hands of the dockyard and all the shipwrights, carpenters and armourers. With his clerk he had to start the bureaucracy of running a ship: the muster roll had to be completed and every two months a copy sent off to the Navy Board; the Admiralty also needed copies every two months of the captain's journal, a daily diary of what was done in the ship and, when at sea, noon positions, what was sighted, the winds experienced and sails carried – as well as events like the flogging of a man. Copies of the Plymouth Port Admiral's orders were needed; copies of more than a hundred forms had to be drawn from the commissioner's office: the port admiral needed a daily report of progress of the work on board the ship.

Life became a little easier a few days later, on 6 January 1799, when Thomas Mills joined as the purser: the responsibility for getting on board and issuing provisions, clothing (known as slops) and tobacco was now his, and once the men could buy their tobacco and be assured of regular provisions, life became much easier.

Proby issued his 'standing orders', which was a list of how he wanted certain evolutions carried out, and how he planned the daily routine of the ship. As soon as Lieutenant Niven was given a copy of the captain's standing orders he made sure that the second lieutenant, master's mates and midshipmen made their copies.

But the *Danae* was far from ready for sea: she had a little more than a couple of dozen men towards her complement, which the Navy Board had settled as 155. However, as a start an entry was made in the muster roll: 'Began wages and sea victualling at whole allowance of all species at Plymouth 12 December, 1798.' This was the date that Lord Proby had read himself in.

By the end of March 1799, when the *Danae* had been in commission for three and a half months, she had received a total of seventy-one seamen and petty officers, and their origins, revealed by the muster roll, are interesting but typical of one of the King's ships at this time. Thirty-four were English, twenty-one Irish, two Welsh and three Scots. The only surprising thing at this stage is that she had so few men claiming to be Americans; she was to have many more of them once she was at sea on patrol, and they were to get the credit or blame for much of her strange history.

The position of Americans, after seven years of war, was still a vexed one. By 1799, no man over twenty-four years of age had been born an American subject, since the Declaration of Independence dated only from 1776. There was no such thing as a birth certificate, and proof of birth depended on the sworn statement of a respectable citizen holding an official position. No American accent had developed, and the British government considered that most men claiming to be American had in fact been born British subjects. The British government's attitude was that one could not avoid the obligations of birth by merely *claiming* the nationality of another country; nationality, like skin, was something with which you were born.

What in fact happened was that British ships of war stopped ships on the high seas and impressed any men they considered to be British. Some of these men had American 'Protections' which, they claimed, proved they were American subjects. They were usually ignored by officers in charge of press gangs, but if the possessor of one could get to an American consul his representations usually resulted in the man's release.

The main problems were twofold. To start with, since birth certificates were then unknown in America, no American could own a legal document proving he was born in a certain place on a certain date. The only document he could carry was a 'Protection'. This was issued by an American Customs collector or consul abroad and it carried the man's name, what age he seemed and a vague physical description. It also stated where the man claimed to come from – the town or village, and state. It was a document saying that a man said he was a certain person and came from a certain place.

The important thing, as far as the British government was concerned, was that the man had provided no proof: it was sufficient just to call at a Customs office or consulate and ask for a Protection, which would be filled in, signed and issued. Not surprisingly, any British seaman finding himself in an American

# CONSULATE OF THE UNITED STATES
## OF
# AMERICA, IN LISBON.

I THOMAS BULKELEY, Conful of the United States of America in the city of Lisbon, DO HEREBY CERTIFY that *Samuel Higgins* an American Seaman, aged *twenty five* years, or thereabouts, of the height of *five* feet *_____* inches, *_____ Complexion _____* blue eyes, common nose a native of the County & town of *Hadden* in the State of Connecticut

Gratis

has this day produced to me proof, in the manner directed in the Act intitled " An Act for the Relief and Protection of American Seamen ; " — and, purfuant to the faid Act, I DO HEREBY CERTIFY that the faid *Samuel Higgins* is a citizen of the United States of America.

IN WITNESS whereof, I have hereunto fet my hand, and affixed the Confular Seal of faid States, DONE in the Office of faid Confulate, in Lisbon the *twenty seventh* day of *December* One thoufand feven hundred and ninety *eight*

*Thomas Bulkeley*

The American Protection form which was produced at a court martial. (Courtesy of Public Record Office, ADM 1/5356) port (usually while serving in a merchant ship) took the precaution of getting himself a Protection on the basis that one never knew when it might come in useful: when a Royal Navy boat came alongside at sea with a press gang for instance, or if the man was seized in the street of an English town or village, a Protection might turn the trick. But because the details required by the Customs officer or consul were vague (for example, 'aged about twenty-five, brown hair, of medium height') they fitted a number of men and the prudent seaman collected a Protection from every port he visited, because Protections could be sold for a good price.

So two types of men had Protections: genuine seamen from America – those probably starting off serving in American ships, or in British and French ships, because at the beginning of the war there were not many American ships at sea; and Britons who had visited America and called on a Customs officer or, more likely, bought a Protection from someone else at the going rate.

The British authorities, whether in the shape of the Admiralty or a ship's officer at the head of a press gang, therefore cast a doubtful eye on a Protection. But at the same time quite a number of genuine Americans were serving voluntarily in the Royal Navy. Pay in a merchant ship was higher, admittedly, but because of dishonest masters there was no guarantee that a seaman always received it. There are hundreds of recorded cases of men being cheated out of all or part of the pay due to them at the end of a voyage. A favourite trick on the part of a corrupt master was claiming against a seaman for damage to the ship or cargo because of alleged carelessness.

Life was hard in the Royal Navy but the sea can be rough and the weather harsh whatever ship a man is in, and for all its disadvantages a man in the Royal Navy received every penny of pay due to him. Also there was always the chance of prize money if an enemy ship was captured, with head money for every prisoner taken. The reason for most men's dislike of serving in the Royal Navy was firstly the discipline, second the poor pay, and third that they were not free to change ships at the end of a voyage. This last disadvantage was more apparent than real: a merchant seaman had to sign on and serve in a ship in order to receive wages, but in fact he probably served continuously, although he might well change ships every six months or so.

The problem of American citizenship was never satisfactorily solved, and was one of the major reasons for the war of 1812. On the one hand the British would not recognize the vagueness of Protections and they could be bought and sold; on the other the United States never paid any attention to the fact that for much of the time Britain was fighting alone against a nation which occupied much of Europe. Napoleon, like the Kaiser and Hitler after him, intended to rule the world.

However, by the end of March 1799 the *Danae* had only two men on board claiming to be Americans, and neither attempted to get in touch with an American consul to secure his release.

In the muster roll the second column after the date when a man joined the ship was headed 'Vol or Prest'. A seaman could either be a volunteer or a pressed man, but the 'vol' or 'prest' noted against the man's name was not always a fair indication. A man was paid a bounty of £5 on joining the Royal Navy at this time – the equivalent of almost five months' pay. When a man was pressed – picked up in streets by a press gang, turned over to a press gang from a jail or a local court as the alternative to going to prison, or taken from a merchant ship – he was always given the chance of 'volunteering', so that he received the bounty. Only the most stubborn of men would reject the bounty and be described in the muster roll as 'prest'. It made no difference to a man's service: a volunteer seaman was treated in the same way as a pressed one, only he was £5 richer.

## CHAPTER FIVE

# THE JERSEY
# FLOTILLA

During January and February 1799, everyone on board the *Danae* was busy preparing the ship for sea. Although at that time no one knew what her orders would be, when she left Plymouth she could be away for three months, and for the whole of that time would have to be completely independent of the land. The ship's company would depend on salt beef and salt pork for meat; there would be fresh vegetables for as long as they lasted (with onions and the like keeping best), and in the flour and rice weevils would flourish.

The meat (generally known as 'salt tack') was kept in large casks, and on the outside of the cask the Admiralty contractor had painted what was often an optimistic description of the number of pieces it contained. When a cask was opened it was emptied with the master watching the cook and his mate, counting the number of pieces, and the master would note in his log what was stencilled on the outside of the cask and the number of pieces actually in it. The meat was then steeped – left to soak for 24 hours to remove some of the salt, which glistened on the meat like a glaze. Beef kept its taste longer than pork but both were bland, leaving the seamen longing for a strong taste, which they usually assuaged by chewing tobacco.

Water was one of the most important items and captains tried to fill the butts at the last moment, so that it would keep longer. Beer was carried to issue to the men in place of water but it was not the stout stuff that yeomen drank in ale houses; instead it was small beer and used only because weak beer lasted a great deal longer than fresh water.

The *Danae* was still very short of men. Following the surgeon on 28 December and the purser on 6 January, the chaplain, Thomas Allsop, arrived on 9 January. No ship under a certain size had to carry a chaplain unless one applied specially. Either Allsop made an application to join the *Danae* or Lord Proby particularly asked for one, because it was not usual for a 20-gun ship to carry a chaplain.

The ship had to make do without a master until the middle of February, throwing a good deal of extra work on to the shoulders of the first lieutenant, Charles Niven, because in port the master was usually responsible for masts, yards, rigging and sails, and in the *Danae*'s case this entailed a considerable amount of work. Thomas Stokes joined the ship as master on 18 February, with a warrant signed by the port admiral.

Lord Proby was finding that not having a master-at-arms with his present crew was difficult. The master-at-arms was in effect the ship's policeman, and on 9 January Proby wrote to Evan Nepean, the Secretary to the Board: 'Please to acquaint my Lords Commissioners of the Admiralty that no master-at-arms has been appointed to His Majesty's ship *Danae* under my command, and move them in favour of Andrew Flynn, who has been doing duty on board of her as such ever since the ship has been commissioned and whom I think in every respect deserving of that situation.' Such a recommendation was enough for their Lordships and a warrant for Flynn was sent down to Plymouth.

Communications between the Admiralty and all the ports used by the King's ships were at this time excellent and far better than the postal service that was to exist nearly two centuries later. Every night, at set times, messengers left the Admiralty on horseback carrying the correspondence for individual ports. The messenger for Portsmouth, for instance, usually arrived there before dawn next day.

Lord Proby's next letter to the Admiralty was in the nature of a protest: their Lordships, it seemed, had not realized just how small and cramped was the *Danae*. Proby wrote to Nepean:

As General Maitland is come down here (by the desire, I understand, of My Lords Commissioners of the Admiralty) to take a passage aboard in His Majesty's ship *Danae*, I beg you will humbly represent to their Lordships that she is not suited to accommodate more than her own officers, so great a part of her provisions is now obliged to be kept in the 'tween decks, for want of room in the hold, that no berth [Proby's clerk wrote 'birth'] can be made for General Maitland and his suite without turning the people upon decks; as to his living in my cabin, there is hardly room if I give it up myself; and to convince their Lordships that I do not make difficulties I have put on the opposite side the dimensions of it.

On the other side of the page he had written:

|  | Feet |  |  |
|---|---|---|---|
| Height | 5 |  |  |
| Breadth forward | 12 |  |  |
| Do. aft | 8' | 6½ inches |  |
| Length | 9 | 10 |  |

That letter, dated 30 January, was considered by the Board on 1 February.* Needless to say the Admiralty changed its mind when it considered the box in which Brigadier General Maitland would have to live for the whole of his passage to Santo Domingo – for that was where Maitland and his staff were bound.

The *Danae* finally sailed from Plymouth at the beginning of March. She had been lying alongside a hulk until she was ready to get under way, and her first voyage under Proby's command was a very short one – higher up the river to the powder magazine, which was isolated from all other buildings and, as a contemporary guide recorded, 'erected with every precaution, to prevent accidents by fire or lightning'. Having loaded powder in her magazine and powder room, the *Danae* then sailed on 2 March. Proby had received orders to join the flotilla based on the Channel Islands and operating against the French coast between the mouth of the Seine and Ushant.

This stretch of the coast is swept by strong currents – in many places the tidal stream reaches six knots and, in some places, eight. Most of the coast westward towards Ushant is backed by steep

---

* In the late 1980s the General Post Office would not dare guarantee that a letter posted in Plymouth would reach a desk in Whitehall, London, within 48 hours.

cliffs and fronted by isolated half-tide rocks, on to which a becalmed ship was easily swept by the tidal stream. It was a coast for skilled seamen, as anyone who has sailed it will testify; captains needed to know when to anchor in thick fog or how to claw off a lee shore under double-reefed courses in a westerly gale. Proby was, fortunately, a good seaman. Nevertheless, he had one fault: he was too slack and trusting with his ship's company. But he lacked nothing in seamanship: one could not command a ship for more than a year along this coast, winter and summer, without a fair measure of technical competence.

The *Danae* arrived at St Helier, the main port in Jersey, where Proby put himself under the command of the senior officer, Captain Philip d'Auvergne, the Prince of Bouillon, but the ship was still only half-manned. She was supposed to have a complement of 155 – the number the Navy Board had decided was necessary to sail and fight the ship effectively. At this time very few of the King's ships had their full complement of men, but few sailed with only half. The *Danae* had seventy-seven warrant and petty officers and men, with four commission officers (Second Lieutenant Robert Stevens had arrived on board to command the Marine detachment). This almost disastrous shortage of men was Proby's nightmare all the time that he commanded the ship.

The task of Captain Philip d'Auvergne, who commanded the flotilla in the Channel Islands, was simple to describe but more difficult to carry out. The ports along the French coast like St Malo, Dieppe, Roscoff, Brest, Rochefort and as far south as Bordeaux and Bayonne were the home of privateers. These ships sailed out into the Channel, often carrying few guns but many men for boarding, and tried to capture British merchant ships, especially those just reaching England with a rich cargo from the West or East Indies. Such ships were supposed to sail in convoys, but the captains of merchant ships were individualists and a convoy of necessity comprised many ships (a hundred was not unusual) of vastly different sizes, speeds and sailing abilities. In bad weather or poor visibility ships often lost or quit the convoy, never to find it again, so that they arrived off the English coast alone – and thus providing a good catch for a French privateer.

The main French fleet was at Brest, nominally blockaded there by a British fleet under the command of Lord Bridport, who had once been a fine officer but was now an old man, troubled by rheumatism and with none of the fire in his belly required of such a commander-in-chief. The result was that the Channel Fleet made occasional forays to the French coast, rattling the bars off Brest, but the main work, since the French Fleet showed no sign of wanting to leave Brest, was catching privateers and, equally important, catching the French coastal trade that carried cargoes between French ports.

Always short of horses and carts and bedevilled with poor roads and long distances, the French naturally preferred to send what men and goods they could by sea. The quickest way of sending several tons of materials from, say, St Malo to Brest was by sea. But it was at sea that the British had their only chance of intercepting such traffic, and it was the task of Captain d'Auvergne to send his motley collection of vessels to the best positions to do this. Coastal traffic had, because of off-lying rocks and shoals, to keep five miles or more offshore, and it was here that the British cruisers waited.

Further to the south-west captains like Edward Pellew kept watch for ships making a dash to the West Indies or, returning from there, trying to get into Brest or Rochefort. But people like Pellew tended to command bigger ships, based on Plymouth, which stayed on patrol for three months at a time and which could – since there were usually two or three in company – give a good account of themselves if they met a French ship of the line (the *Droits de l'Homme* for example). D'Auvergne's flotilla, therefore, usually comprised smaller ships, ones which could get close in to the numerous bays along the Brittany coast yet which were weatherly enough to fight their way off a lee shore when a sudden gale blew up out of nowhere – the coast was famous for them, and the Channel Islands ports provided little shelter.

For any eager young officer like Proby, command of the *Danae* on such a station was the kind of exciting life of which he had dreamed. It is important to realize that at this time war was something left to the professionals. Conscription for the Army and pressing for the Navy certainly existed, but the average man did not feel any need (or any pressures) to volunteer for the Navy or Army. Young men frequented the fashionable drawing rooms and no hostess thought for a moment that they should be serving the King. Proby was thus very different from the usual run of young men born into his social position. As the Earl of Carysfort's eldest son, and with a courtesy title, he could have lived the life of his contemporaries. His father was Member of Parliament for the Lincolnshire constituency of Stamford and had a comfortable country home at Elton Hall, while in London he had a town house in Stanhope Street. There was nothing to stop Lord Proby (who celebrated his twentieth birthday on 19 June, three months after arriving in the Channel Islands with the *Danae*) from spending his time hunting across the rolling fields of Huntingdonshire – Elton Hall had ample stables – or gambling or spending his time at receptions and balls.

Instead he had deliberately chosen life at sea, forgoing comfortable drawing rooms and the company of pretty young women to live in a cabin with five feet headroom and no social life. All he had was the entire responsibility for the safety and handling of one of the King's ships and the lives of several score men. And, of course, the excitement of war against the French. For the previous five years he had been almost continuously at sea and, as a lieutenant, he had served under Sir John Jervis, reckoned one of the best men under whom a young officer could serve.

But however good a seaman he was and however good a ship handler, Proby had more than his share of the irritations of command. The *Danae* had not been in the Channel Islands for a fortnight before he was having to write to the Admiralty again. With his ship anchored in Granville Bay, on the French coast south-east of Jersey, he wrote to William Marsden, the first secretary under Evan Nepean:

> The boatswain of the *Danae* having (without leave) absented himself so long as to oblige me to run him on the books [i.e. put 'R' against his name on the muster roll] the Prince of Bouillon at my request has find [sic] Mr David Irons (boatswain of the *Brave*) in the vacancy, he bears uncommon good character both as a seaman and an officer; could you forward the confirmation of his acting order you add much to the obligation I am already under to you.

Until Irons arrived on board from the *Brave* (a 12-gun hired lugger commanded by Lieutenant John Guyon), William White, a thirty-eight-year-old bosun's mate from Alton, in Hampshire, had been acting as bosun since February the previous year.

Then on 4 April, as if to make up for the irritation of having to run one boatswain and watch another as he settled in, Proby made his first capture. He was cruising off the eleven-mile-wide shoal of the Îles Chausey, close to Granville Bay, when lookouts sighted a lugger and Proby gave the order to chase. The private signal was hoisted and it was a challenge to which any vessel in Captain d'Auvergne's command would have the answer, but the lugger did not reply. The chase started a quarter of the way between the French coast at Granville and Jersey, and the *Danae* quickly caught her. She was the French lugger *Le Sans Quartier*, carrying 14 guns, and despite her fearsome name she surrendered without a fight. Proby took off all the Frenchmen as prisoners, giving the *Danae*'s Marine lieutenant, Robert Stevens, and his men (the *Danae* carried sixteen Marine privates, two corporals, one sergeant and a drummer boy) their first task against the enemy.

Proby put a prize crew on board and sent her into St Helier, from where she was sent to Plymouth. It meant that Proby lost a midshipman and some men until they could return to the *Danae*, but at last he had opened his account with the prize agent he had appointed to handle the *Danae*'s captures, whether *Le Sans Quartier* was bought into the Royal Navy or sold off at auction in England to a private buyer. Either way the prize agent would receive the money and eventually distribute it to the men of the frigate.

Proby now had three midshipmen on board, and although by tradition the life of a midshipman was always hard in one of the King's ships these three were particularly cramped on board the *Danae*. But apart from being helpful assistants to the officer of the deck, they were always useful as prizemasters. When one of the enemy was captured and had to be sent into a British port, it was usual for a midshipman to be given a handful of men (the minimum needed to sail the ship), a chart (if he was lucky, otherwise he hurriedly made a copy of one the master was using) or a course to steer and expected to deliver his charge, returning to the ship as quickly as possible after notifying the prize agent and making sure none of his men deserted.

The first midshipman had joined the ship the day that Lord Proby commissioned her. He was Richard Waddy, a twenty-year-old Irishman from Dublin. He was the *Danae*'s only midshipman until the ship arrived in the Channel Islands, when John Derric, aged twenty-six, was sent over from the *Brave* lugger on the orders of Captain d'Auvergne. Derrie would have found his berth in the *Danae* spacious compared with the lugger. He was almost certainly a young man who had either failed his examination for lieutenant, which he would have taken when he was twenty, or had passed but lacked the luck or influence to get an appointment as a lieutenant.

The third midshipman to join the ship had the distinction of having his name spelled two different ways in two successive copies of the *Danae*'s muster rolls and subsequent court martial proceedings. Archibald Herron (or Heron) was twenty years old when he joined the ship and came from Edinburgh, his accent being the counterpoint to the Irish lilt of Waddy.

With a month to go to his twentieth birthday, Lord Proby's trouble with his carpenter, John Chubb, came to a head. Chubb had been a nuisance ever since he joined the ship, careless in his work, careless with carpenters' tools, useless at controlling his carpenter's crew, and never producing the required regular reports for the captain. Finally, in the Channel Islands, he did something which Proby did not describe but which led him, on 6 May, to give Chubb the choice: face a court martial or resign his warrant.

Chubb seems to have had little doubt which way a court martial verdict would go and chose to resign his warrant. Proby made him write out his letter of resignation and from the wording there is little doubt that he dictated it. 'Sir,' Chubb wrote to Evan Nepean. 'I have to request that you will be pleased to acquaint my Lords Commissioners of the Admiralty of my wish to resign my warrant as carpenter of His Majesty's ship *Danae*, and move their Lordships to comply therewith.' Proby wrote a covering letter to Nepean the same day: 'I beg you will lay the enclosed letters before my Lords Commissioners of the Admiralty. The one to William Sanders will lay open Mr Chubb's reason for wishing to resign and sufficiently convince their Lordships of his incapacity as an officer.'

The Sanders letter is not in the Admiralty records and he was not employed by the Admiralty or Navy Board. For the usually courteous Proby to omit the customary 'Mr' makes one think he was somehow involved in Chubb's misdeed without being a member of the *Danae*'s ship's company.

Nepean wrote on the reverse side of Lord Proby's letter their Lordships' decision in the case of John Chubb: 'May 14. Lord Proby to be directed to acquaint John Chubb their Lordships have no objection to [him] resigning his warrant as carpenter but they will not permit him to be discharged from the Service.' The Royal Navy was always short of men – one of the reasons that seamen guilty of serious crimes were usually flogged rather than hanged – and the Admiralty was not going to let Chubb become a free man as a result of choosing to resign his warrant instead of being court-martialled.

Chubb resigning his warrant did not bring an end to the affair, and three weeks later Proby wrote again to Nepean from St Helier. 'Mr Chubb never having taken his warrant from the clerk of the checque's office, I suppose his signifying (as he has done) his wish to resign is sufficient. I have therefore to request that their Lordships will be pleased to appoint another carpenter to the *Danae* and let me know their pleasure respecting Mr Chubb.'

June passed and on 24 July Proby wrote yet again to the Admiralty, telling Nepean: 'I beg you will acquaint their Lordships that no carpenter having been appointed to the *Danae*, to supersede John Chubb (who had their permission to resign his warrant some time ago) the stores are of course still in his care, and I am afraid he is not a very fit person for such a charge; the ship being without a carpenter is not in a state of refitting should any accident happen at sea.'

Proby's later letter describing his motives shows that, for a young man one month past his twentieth birthday, he had considerable understanding of human nature, even if his humanity was in this and subsequent cases somewhat misguided. Anyway, another month passed and still Proby was not rid of Chubb. He wrote to the Admiralty yet again on 26 August, three months and three weeks after the confrontation with the man:

Chubb (the late carpenter of the *Danae*) is still on board her. My reason for pressing their Lordships to appoint another carpenter was: first that the ship is not safe without a person in that position and secondly, Chubb is not fit to be entrusted with the stores, but if I take them out of his charge before he is superseded, the other duties which I am bound to execute would make it impossible for me to prevent embezzlement or misapplication of the stores.

My motive in allowing Chubb to avoid a court martial by resigning was merely a motive of humanity, that by the little knowledge there would be of his disgrace he might still have a chance of repairing his fortune by future good behaviour, and I all along considered it as a thing of course: that in resigning his warrant he would return to the position he was in, before his promotion to the *Danae*.

In many ways the *Danae* was like a bucket into which water dripped. In time the bucket would fill and start overflowing. Although no one could have guessed it at the time, a man joined the ship on 1 July (the next muster roll recorded it as 2 July) who was to have a great effect on the bucket. The details were quite usual: a volunteer, giving his place of birth as Liverpool, his age as twenty-four, and his name as William Jackson. Because of his experience he was put down as an able seaman – 'rated able'.

Judging by his later actions, Jackson was a brooding man, able to keep his thoughts and plans to himself and bide his time. He did his duty without ever getting into trouble; he never 'hoarded his tot' of rum, keeping his twice-daily issue until he had enough to get drunk. For months, until he reached what he considered the appropriate moment, Jackson was a good able seaman: the type of man of whom the *Danae* was always short.

The problem of the *Danae*'s carpenter might have been thought to have been solved when John Chubb left the ship and a new carpenter, John Heaton, arrived on board at Plymouth on 23 September. A few days later, Lord Proby had to write from Plymouth Sound to the Admiralty about him, requesting Evan Nepean: 'I beg you will inform my Lords Commissioners of the Admiralty that on the eleventh of October John Heaton was (with a good deal of difficulty) brought on board, without having taken up his warrant [from the clerk of the checque's office] and so drunk that he could not be entrusted on shore to do it then . . .'

Starting off with William Johnston, who had deserted and was replaced by Chubb, who was replaced by Heaton, Lord Proby and the *Danae* had more than their share of bad luck with carpenters . . .

The Admiralty then appointed Thomas Davies, who joined the

ship on 26 October. Although Davies was to prove a satisfactory carpenter, he joined the ship on the same day as a group of other men, seamen, who were to help the *Danae*'s bucket overflow.

A few weeks earlier, before returning to Plymouth for a refit, Proby had attempted to get the position of his master-at-arms regularized, so he wrote to Nepean:

> I beg you will be so good as to move their Lordships to sign a warrant for Bartholomew Quin, who has been serving duty as master-at-arms of the *Danae* for some time past with great diligence and sobriety.
>
> In consequence of a complaint made against the late master-at-arms, their Lordships signified, through you, their desire that I should recommend some person fit for the situation, and they would appoint him to supersede Andrew O'Flynn [*sic*]. I mentioned Bartholomew Quin and you acquainted [me] in answer that 'Their Lordships have signed a warrant for Andrew Flynn and desire me to discharge the late master-at-arms into the first guardship I meet.' This must be a mistake which I beg you to rectify.

Written diagonally across the bottom left-hand corner of the letter – the customary way in which the Board Secretary recorded the Board's decision after raising the matter of the letter with them – was: 'See Captain Proby's letter on this subject: his former letter was sent to the Board Room.' A further note added: 'August 10, it appears a mistake in the office by sending a warrant for the man who was to be suspended, A. Flynn. The warrant should be for Bartholomew Quin. No warrant has been sent, nor have I seen anything on the subject before, the mistake must lay in the Common Letter Branch, in answer to Lord Proby's letter. No mistake can be there as the letter alluded to was written from a minute made on Lord Proby's letter.'

Proby finally received Quin's warrant, so that the errant Flynn could revert to being an ordinary seaman and Quin, who had been acting as master-at-arms although only rated on the ship's books as an able seaman, could get 'the rate for the job', an entry being made beside his name on the muster roll: 'Master-at-Arms per warrant 12 August 1799.'

## CHAPTER SIX

# THE CHANNEL FLEET

*T*hroughout the spring and early summer of 1799, the *Danae* regularly sailed from Jersey with orders from Captain d'Auvergne to patrol a particular part of the coast. Proby became very familiar with the most inhospitable coast either side of the Channel. Cap Fréhel, Sables d'Or, St Brieuc, Binic, Bréhec, Paimpol and the off-lying Île de Bréhat – along with the Roches Douvres almost twenty miles offshore: these were the names constantly appearing in the *Danae*'s log and captain's journal.

The constant tacking and wearing, reefing and furling, strong winds and sails slatting meant that by autumn the *Danae* had to return to Plymouth for a refit. The *Medway* hulk was moored in Plymouth Sound and the *Danae*, instead of anchoring, went alongside her. The entries in Proby's journal then give a good picture of life on board. Although it was hard work for the men, their food was better. Every three or four days a boat came out from the dockyard with fresh beef, giving the men a welcome rest from 'salt tack'.

All the *Danae*'s guns were hoisted out and swayed over to the hulk so that carriages and slides could be inspected for rot and then painted. The guns were given a coat of blacking and the splices on the train tackles and breechings were checked. The heavy anchor cables were roused out of the cable tiers and ranged along the deck so that they could be inspected for chafe. At the same time the standing and running rigging was inspected, several shrouds being replaced and others sent down to have seizings renewed and occasionally turned end for end, when there was not sufficient wear to condemn the whole rope.

On Friday, 11 October, at Plymouth Proby noted in his journal:

'Received beer and water, men employed as before.' Next day as a result of some rope being condemned, came the entry: 'Men working up junk,' which meant unreeving the rope and making it up into short lengths which could be used as bag o' wrinkle, the thick woven strand wrapped round rigging to prevent sails chafing.

Saturday was the usual busy day on board the *Danae* and of course gave no hint that the events of the next day were going to be the most significant in the history of the frigate. On Sunday, as men began painting the ship it began to rain and a little later a boat from the frigate *Révolutionnaire* brought over six men for the *Danae*. All six men called themselves Americans and one of them was black. They had just been captured from the French privateer *Bordelais*, which had been taken by the *Révolutionnaire*, whose commander, Captain Thomas Twysden, was very doubtful about them: he considered they might be English, in which case they should be court-martialled as traitors in the employ of the enemy. Eventually he let himself be persuaded and obviously had no regrets when ordered to send some men to the *Danae*.

Lord Proby later recalled that the six men 'called themselves Americans; they declared they were forced to serve the French and as there was nothing to prove they were English I took them to fill the *Danae*'s complement which was at that time very short.' The fact that Proby accepted that they were Americans meant he was six men better off – two able seamen and four ordinary seamen. However, obviously Proby had some doubts:

> Every necessary measure was adopted to prevent any ill consequences arising from their bad dispositions; the midshipmen were put in a berth between the fore and main hatchways and all the officers had orders to watch these men narrowly but they behaved extremely well, till I was obliged to go to sea with a large proportion of the most attentive petty officers and near thirty of the best men absent in prizes; this opportunity they must have grasped to propagate principles which it is well known are but too easily adopted by men who seldom weigh the difference between unlicensed anarchy and the possession of real social liberty.

Proby was, alas, talking with the benefit of hindsight. He was to regret that Captain Twysden did not bring the men to trial after taking them off the *Bordelais*.

Although Proby referred to all six of them claiming to be Americans, in fact one of them said he was French. The *Danae*'s muster roll by chance listed the worst man's name first: John Williams II was an able seaman who claimed to come from Boston and be twenty-nine years old (the first John Williams in the *Danae* was a twenty-year-old ordinary seaman, a volunteer from Scarborough).

The next man from the *Bordelais* was John Brown III, a black claiming to be from Virginia and twenty-six years old. Samuel Scarborough, twenty years old and an ordinary seaman, said he too was from Virginia while the fourth man was David Greig, also an ordinary seaman who said he came from Charleston, South Carolina. Charles Goodrough, twenty-six years old, said he was from France, but it was not unusual for a Frenchman to be serving in the Royal Navy, it being assumed that such a man was a monarchist or had other good reasons for leaving his native country.

The sixth of the draft sent over from *La Révolutionnaire* was the fifth put down in the *Danae*'s muster roll as an American and the third who told the clerk filling in the details that he was from Virginia. He was twenty-one years old and yet another Brown, only this time James, but he was listed 'the Second' because the first, an Irishman, had been serving in the *Danae* before she was commissioned.

The day after the men from the *Bordelais* privateer arrived on board the rain continued, interrupting the painting, and the boat came out from the dockyard with more fresh beef. This had been one of the results of the great mutiny at the Nore and Spithead in 1797: the men had demanded that they be served fresh meat while in port, and in turn it was now something about which the Admiralty was very punctilious.

By Wednesday most of the painting and the work on the rigging was completed and the guns were hoisted back on board and lowered into their slides. The stunsail yards were hoisted up and the firebooms and spare yards were stowed. By Thursday the men were bending on the staysails and, Proby noted in his journal, 'getting ready for sea'. Friday saw the men 'employed as before' and more fresh beef arrived. The cable was bent on to the bower anchor on Saturday and the topgallant yards were sent up, so that the *Danae*'s masts looked less like bare trees. The sails were bent on to the yards and the sheets and braces rove.

By now the task of preparing the ship for sea was speeding up and on 20 October, with the wind down to little more than light airs, the pilot came on board after lunch. Proby's journal records, 'At 2 cast ship off; made all sail, pilot came to in Sound. Anchored with best bower [anchor]. Employed getting ready for sea.'

But even the brief sail from alongside the *Medway* hulk round into the Sound had emphasized just how short of men Proby was. He was hoping to join Lord Bridport's Channel Fleet, which would mean that all sail orders had to be executed smartly – smart ship handling was the measure of a captain's ability – and there was always the chance of action. Fighting the ship while manoeuvring her would be beyond Proby's capability if he was critically short of topmen, reducing him to the heartbreaking choice of whether to have men at the guns or at the sheets, tacks, braces and out on the yards.

So Proby made a decision which must have seemed very routine at the time but, like receiving the six former *Bordelais* men from *La Révolutionnaire*, was eventually to have a disastrous result. He noted in his journal, 'armed our boats and sent them on impress service.'

Pressing men in these circumstances was indeed a routine task. In Plymouth Sound merchant ships just arrived in convoys from places like the West Indies waited: for another convoy to a different port, or for orders from their owners, telling them where their cargo was to be unloaded. Frequently a ship would leave the West Indies in convoy, laden with sugar, molasses, hides or spices, and have no idea of her eventual destination: she would be bound for Plymouth 'for orders', and on arriving would be told that the shippers wanted the cargo taken round to London, or Liverpool, or Bristol ... At the same time a convoy bound for the East or West Indies, India or the Cape might be assembling in Plymouth, so that for three or four weeks, depending on wind and weather, merchant ships would be arriving from various other ports, to meet their escorts and sail.

All the time that such ships were anchored they were liable to be boarded by a press gang (and, of course, they could be stopped at sea, too). Then the officer in charge of the press gang was subject to few rules. Officers and apprentices could not be pressed, and he had to leave enough men on board to work the ship. Thus it was better to press from an incoming merchant ship: she would need fewer men to sail round to the port of London, for example, than to cross the Atlantic to Barbados.

So the *Danae*'s boats were hoisted out, swivel guns were lowered into them (small guns intended to intimidate argumentative shipmasters rather than control pressed seamen) and, with seamen armed with muskets and cutlasses, the little flotilla under the command of Lieutenant Rollo set off to visit all the merchant ships.

From one ship they might take only a single man, and by the time he returned to the *Danae* Rollo had ten men and two youths. It is unlikely he could have found a more cosmopolitan haul of men, and all of them except one eventually joined in the splashing when the bucket overflowed. Two of the men rated able came from Scotland (Aberdeen and East Lothian), two were Welshmen (one of whom refused to take the bounty and was put down as 'prest', the rest having 'vol' against their names), one came from Liverpool and another (the only loyal man and at forty-five, fifteen years older than most of the others) from Othersford in Yorkshire, while a twenty-seven-year-old able seaman, Christian Helmar, was listed as from Prussia.

Lieutenant Rollo had not neglected to press two youngsters – Thomas Collis, aged seventeen and from Dursley in Gloucestershire, was put down as a boy, 3rd class, while Sam Frankmore, a year or two older, became a boy, 2nd class. With the one exception mentioned, all these men and those six from the *Révolutionnaire* were to become traitors.

There was yet another change among the *Danae*'s senior men, and Samuel Giles, the ship's clerk, recorded that the boatswain David Irons, sent on board at St Helier by Captain d'Auvergne, was transferred to the *Triton*, and in his place the *Danae* received John Hollowood as boatswain.

On Monday, 21 October, the day after receiving an extra dozen men and boys, the *Danae* received more provisions from the dockyard. Her boats brought out bread, butter, beef and cheese, while Proby's journal recorded: 'men working up junk.' The next day the *Danae* took on powder from the magazine and Proby was lucky because it poured with rain the day after and the men had to stay below 'working up junk'. The next day they spent scrubbing hammocks and the day after brought fresh breezes so that the hammocks dried, and at noon the ship 'fired salute of 21 guns in commemoration of His Majesty's Accession to the Throne'.

On Saturday Proby received word that some Jersey privateers had arrived at Torpoint and immediately sent over a party to see if he could get any men for the *Danae*. The boat came back with five, four of whom were put down in the muster roll as able seamen. The fifth man, an ordinary seaman, refused to take the bounty and was listed as 'prest'. Once again, Proby was unlucky: when the time came, three out of the five were to be traitors.

The next few days were busy with receiving more stores and men were 'employed stowing away'. By Thursday the weather had turned bad and strong winds were blowing across the Sound. There were heavy squalls and rain and Proby ordered the topmasts to be sent down to reduce the windage. But the wind increased and in the squalls the *Danae* was being laid over so that, as Proby recorded in his log next day, 'struck lower yards and got topgallants masts on deck.'

On the third day, Saturday, 2 November, with the wind still screaming across the Sound and all ships snubbing viciously at their anchor cables, 'answered signal for all launches to go to the assistance of a ship in distress. Sent an officer in the cutter to her assistance.' It was as much as the men in the cutter could do to make any headway against both wind and sea, with the ever present danger of broaching, and Proby noted, 'boat returned, not being able to approach ship.'

The weather did not improve, and there was still a gale blowing on 5 November, when the journal recorded: 'Fired a salute in commemoration of Gunpowder Treason.'

A few days later, with the ship nearly ready for sea, Proby was given orders to join Lord Bridport's Channel Fleet, which was preparing for a cruise off Brest. Proby considered that there was very little professional advancement to be gained in serving in the flotilla based on Jersey: advancement would only come to men who could shine under the eye of the Admiral.

On the basis of 'out of sight, out of mind', he was probably right, and Proby wrote to Lord Bridport on 15 November the kind of letter that most officers wrote on being appointed to a fleet: 'My Lord, I congratulate myself very heartily in at last succeeding in getting orders to join the Channel Fleet under your Lordship's command. I shall sail early tomorrow morning 16 November if the wind will permit, and I hope I shall be able by my diligence to convince you that the kindness you have shown me since I had the honour of being presented to you, has not been thrown away.'

The last few days before sailing were hectic. On Sunday, 10 November, the *Danae*'s boats were still bringing out stores although the wind was freshening and making rowing across the Sound extremely hard work. By next day heavy squalls brought all boat work to a stop and soon the topgallant masts were being sent down again as the ship rolled violently and then Proby ordered the lower yards to be struck.

Tuesday, 12 November, was no better. The topgallant masts were sent right down on deck and, because the ship was snubbing so violently at her anchors in the heavy seas brought up by the wind, more cable was veered. Nor was it any better on the Wednesday – 'strong gale and squally with rain, working up junk,' Proby's journal recorded. Fortunately the gale blew itself out during the night so that Proby could write next morning, 'hoisted sails to dry.' Later in the day he wrote: 'Furled sails, hove in to one cable on bower, up lower yards and topgallant masts.'

On the 15th, the day he wrote to Lord Bridport, the *Danae* got up her second anchor and hauled in on her best bower. Boats were still going in to the dockyard to bring out beer and water. 'Employed getting ready for sea,' Proby wrote, no doubt excited as he saw several ships of the line and frigates also preparing. This would be the first time since the Mediterranean, when as a lieutenant he commanded the *Peterel* for fourteen months under the eye of Sir John Jervis, that Proby had served directly under an admiral, and the first time ever that he had actually commanded a ship that was actively part of a fleet.

The fleet sailed from Plymouth at daybreak on the 16th with an easterly wind – a stroke of good fortunate appreciated by every commanding officer in the fleet – and Proby was noting in his journal: 'At noon Bolt Head north a half west, distance three miles, light airs and cloudy.' The *Danae* had weighed in the Sound at half past midnight, and actually left at 9 am. In the afternoon the weather had changed abruptly so that by 3 pm the topmen were tying in three reefs. Proby could see Bolt Head to starboard and although the *Danae* was making good progress under triple-reefed topsails, there was no sign of Lord Bridport's fleet. Proby again checked the rendezvous and then at 3.30 pm wrote thankfully, 'At 3.30 saw Fleet, made our number and wore ship on the starboard tack and joined Fleet.'

The wind soon piped up strong enough to force Proby to send down the topgallant yards. (The French Lieutenant Laporte's report that the ship was tender was borne out by the frequency – even at anchor – with which Proby had to send down the topgallant masts and yards.)

The next day Lord Bridport's flagship hoisted the signal for all captains and Proby was rowed over from the *Danae* to meet his new commander-in-chief. Bridport seems to have told his captains what they would have already guessed, that the fleet was going to cruise off Ushant, rattling the bars off the Black Rocks at Brest, where the main French fleet was at anchor.

The boat trip to the flagship and back was a rough and wet trip, and as soon as he was back on board the *Danae* the topmen went aloft. Proby recorded: 'At 5 filled and close reefed topsails.' By noon next day the *Danae*'s log noted that Ushant was twenty-one miles away to the south-east, and the weather rapidly improved during the night so that by the next morning the journal could record: 'Light breezes and clear, up topgallant yards, out 2 and 3 reefs in topsails. At 4 p.m. made signal for strange sail SE by E.'

At last Proby, commanding a frigate (albeit a small one), was at sea with the fleet, his ship fulfilling a frigate's classic role, acting as the admiral's eyes, spotting and investigating strange sail as soon as they came in sight.

Next day the *Danae*'s lookouts spotted two strange sail and Proby ordered the appropriate signals to be made to the flagship, delighted when the signals were acknowledged and he was ordered to investigate. 'Made all sail in chase,' Proby noted. For the next three days the *Danae* continued in company with the fleet, and on Monday, 25 November, she was again investigating a strange sail. This led to the *Danae*'s boat going alongside and boarding the

*Danzig* packet and pressing five men, two of whom refused to take the bounty and were put down as 'prest'.

Proby's best haul of men came a couple of days later, on Wednesday, 27 November, when the *Danae* chased a Jersey privateer and her boat brought fifteen men. However, he could not keep them: before there was time to get their details down in the muster roll a signal from the flagship told him to send eleven men to the *Excellent*. That same afternoon, crowding on sail to investigate another ship just sighted, the *Danae* carried away her larboard foretopmast studding sail boom – not a very disastrous thing to happen, but irritating to a young captain aware that telescopes would be watching from on board the flagship.

On Saturday, with the headland of St Mathieu, at the entrance to Brest, just six miles away to the east, Proby brought to another Jersey privateer and impressed eight men, but for reasons not made clear they were not entered on the muster roll, probably being sent across to other ships. A few hours later a proud Proby noted in his journal: 'Part company with Fleet.'

The area off Brest and the Chenal du Four and Chenal de la Helle between Ushant and the mainland was potentially the most dangerous and exciting in which to command a frigate, and Proby began December as part of a small squadron detached from the fleet and comprising the *Danae*, the 74-gun ship of the line *Excellent* and the 38-gun frigate *Uranie*, having received his orders from Lord Bridport.

However, he was to be parted from the fleet for only a matter of hours, for he found that the *Danae*'s bowsprit was sprung (i.e. split). Fortunately, while the *Danae*'s new carpenter, Thomas Davies, supervised repairs, the *Royal George* sent over provisions. The *Danae* was so cramped that it was impossible to stow enough provisions for a number of men for a long cruise, and Proby had to take every opportunity of stocking up.

By Tuesday, 3 December, with the bowsprit repaired, Proby set off again in company with the *Excellent, Uranie* and the cutter *Lurcher*, and within hours Proby was noting: 'Boarded a sloop from Calais to Bordeaux.' Any French vessel hoping to get down to Bordeaux from Calais would hug the coast, passing as close as possible to Brest, inside Ushant and through the Chenal du Four and Chenal de la Helle, hoping for a fair wind and good visibility.

And that was just where the little squadron was waiting. The captured sloop was sent off to Plymouth with a prize crew.

Nothing was sighted the next day, but then Proby wrote: 'Boarded sloop from Ostend to Nantz [sic: Nantes]. Squadron in company.' Next day, however, much to Proby's annoyance, he had to record: 'Lost sight of squadron.' At noon Ushant was away to the north-east, distant twenty-four miles, with five sails in sight.

For the next few days, until the *Danae* met the *Excellent* again on Saturday, the entries in the journal were almost monotonous – 'Boarded Jersey privateer, impressed 4 men' . . . 'Boarded ship from Embden [sic] to St Martins' . . . and at last: 'Chased two strange sail. Fired two guns, brought them to, they were *Nimrod* and *Lurcher*, cutters.' Within a few hours Proby was able to add: 'Rejoined *Excellent*.'

The next week was unexciting as far as Proby was concerned: on Monday, 16 December, the guns' crews were exercised and the carronades fired under the watchful eye of the gunner, Israel Lewis. Then the men marked down in the watch, quarter and station bill as having pistols or muskets were given a chance of hitting floating targets, and they were followed by Lieutenant Stevens exercising his Marines with muskets, helped by Sergeant Thomas Clark.

The wind was light and the tidal stream strong when the *Danae*, with her comparatively shallow draft, was sent off on her own, and Proby anchored for the night in a quiet bay which he had previously explored when he wanted a sheltered spot in which to anchor the frigate to set up the rigging. Since rope rigging stretched under the constant flexing and tension of the masts, it was necessary every now and again to tighten up the shrouds and stays, and on the 19th the journal reported: 'Anchored . . . to set up rigging fore and aft.'

For the next four nights Proby anchored in the bay, waiting each day for one of the French coasters to pass; then on Christmas Day, weighing at daybreak, the *Danae*'s lookouts soon spotted a ship stranded on the Penmarchs, a series of jagged rocks – she must have gone up during the night. Proby took the *Danae* as close as he dared, recognized the wreck as a British frigate, and then anchored in thirty fathoms (180 feet).

All the *Danae*'s boats were hoisted out and with an officer in each they headed for the wreck. She was the 38-gun frigate *Ethalion*, commanded by Captain John Searle. There was no chance of getting the *Ethalion* off – she would break up in the next westerly gale – and the ship's company's Christmas present was to be rescued by the *Danae*. 'Received officers and ship's company of the *Ethalion*,' Proby noted in his journal and, faced with another 150 extra men on board, he was thankful when two more sail were sighted in the afternoon and they answered the private signal. 'Made sail towards the *Sylph* and a cutter, sent *Ethalion* people on board *Sylph*.' The *Sylph*, of 18 guns, was smaller than the *Danae* and commanded only by a lieutenant, so Proby had the authority to give him orders, backed up by Captain Searle, and she would be in Plymouth within a few hours.

By nightfall on Christmas Day the *Danae* was back on patrol, the hectic rescue of the *Ethalion*'s men soon becoming little more than a reason for the Danaes not being able to celebrate Christmas properly.

It is significant that in Proby's journal for this period, from 10 October until 31 December, not one flogging is recorded. It indicates not that Proby did not flog, but that he did not record it. It would have been common enough for men to hoard their tots of rum for a few days before Christmas, so that they provided some work for the master-at-arms, Bartholomew Quin. Proby ended this particular journal, dated New Year's Eve, 'off Ushant'. He signed it 'Proby' and started a new one – the one he had just completed would, according to the King's Regulations and Admiralty Instructions, be sent in to the Admiralty for their inspection.

It was the last one that the Admiralty ever received from the *Danae*: the new one that Proby now started would end up being thrown into the sea only three months later and less than twenty miles from where it was started.

Proby's excitement at operating off Ushant, intercepting enemy and neutral ships (and with luck being able to impress men from privateers sailing out of Jersey and Guernsey), was soon brought to an end: less than a month after rescuing the *Ethalion*'s men, the little flush deck frigate ran into very bad weather and had to limp into Plymouth Sound, from where he wrote to Evan Nepean on 23 January.

'I beg you will inform my Lords Commissioners of the Admiralty,' he wrote in the usual stylized fashion, 'that his Majesty's ship under my command arrived at this port in consequence of both her main topmasts being badly sprung.' By 'both', Proby must have meant that when one was sprung and sent down, the spare one swayed up in its place was in turn sprung. He continued: 'I enclose an account of her state and the probable time when she will be ready to return upon her station. It would be possible to get her ready in a shorter time than five days, but since the ship's company's wages were due near three months ago, I suppose it will be proper to get them paid now.'

Delaying the ship for the men to be paid the wages they could not receive while they were at sea (they were only paid by the clerk of the checque – in effect the paymaster – in a port set aside for paying wages) was a piece of thoughtfulness on Proby's part, because while they were at sea they could spend money only on slops (the clothes bought from the purser) or tobacco, and in either case the purser gave credit.

Waiting to get the men paid, when a more ambitious man might have hurried everyone to get the ship to sea again, tends to show that Proby was a young man whose fault was perhaps being too kindly; certainly not too harsh. He had tried to save the carpenter Chubb from a court martial when having to put up with the man's behaviour for weeks would have tried the patience of most captains; his eagerness to give a man credit (in letters to the Admiralty concerning men sent to the ship by Captain d'Auvergne) and requesting the promotion of men like Quin indicate a captain who cared for his men. There was none of the harshness and erratic punishment that led to a group of men in the frigate *Hermione* murdering their captain and several officers and carrying the ship into a port on the Spanish Main.

Just as important, Proby handled the *Danae* well, both when serving under Captain d'Auvergne and under Lord Bridport. As mentioned earlier, this north French coast was cliff-girt and scattered with rocks, and swept by strong currents, but the *Danae* (unlike the *Ethalion*) had not come to grief. Sprung topmasts were the fault of wood and weather.

There was a small item of good news to report to Nepean. 'The *Danae* has only retaken the *Providence* sloop from Guernsey to Plymouth since my last letter. I enclose a paper with some intelligence procured from two neutrals boarded the 19th inst.'

The paper, neatly ruled in columns, recorded that the *Altona*, master John Delro, a 60-ton hoy with nine men on board and bound from Lisbon to Copenhagen with salt and fruit, reported that an English frigate* had been lost on the bar at Lisbon, although the crew had been saved. The bar at Lisbon and the strength of the Tagus sweeping across it was a trap for a well-found ship, let alone a clumsy transport.

The other vessel was a 300-ton ship, the *Dorothea* of Hamburg, bound to her home port from Bordeaux with wine and prunes. Her captain reported that there were twenty sail of French privateers at Bordeaux which were ready for sea.

* In fact the 26-gun armed transport *Weymouth*.

## CHAPTER SEVEN

# TRIALS FOR
# TWO CAPTAINS

On 1 January 1800, the day that Lord Proby started his new journal, the *Danae*'s first captain, *Lieutenant de vaisseau* Pierre Laporte, faced a court martial in Rochefort on a charge of losing his ship.

A year and a half had elapsed since Sir Edward Pellew in the *Indefatigable* had captured *La Vaillante* and her pitiful cargo of *déportés*. In the meantime Laporte had been exchanged for a British post captain. The regular exchange of prisoners was by now well established, with a French commissioner, M. Otto, resident in London to help choose the men to be exchanged and arrange for the sailings of the cartel vessels.

Following his brief captivity in England, Laporte had fallen ill. He applied to the Minister of Marine for sick leave and when it was granted went to Bayonne 'to recoup his health', as the Rochefort archives record. Soon after arriving back in France he petitioned the Minister for a court martial to examine his conduct leading up to the capture of *La Vaillante* but was told 'it is necessary to await the witnesses.' This was because most if not all the petty officers and seamen were still prisoners in England, awaiting exchange. French officers were always exchanged quickly because, with few French ships of war at sea, few officers and captains were captured, and the 'balance of exchange' as far as officers were concerned was always in favour of the French.

Finally the exchanges yielded enough witnesses for the Minister to order the *Commandant des Armes* at Rochefort to arrange for the trial to be held. When this began on New Year's Day 1800, at Rochefort, it opened with brief details of the voyage: 'The cruise began on 7 Floréal year 6, the ship left the Isle of Aix roads on

19 Thermidor at 10 o'clock in the morning and was captured on 21 Thermidor.'

The charge against Laporte was then read: 'That by incapacity or negligence he allowed his ship to be captured by the enemy.'

The minutes record that the first witness was 'Jean Perrier, fifty years of age, sailor second class'. Perrier's evidence, recorded in the minutes, was quite straightforward: he saw a ship about fourteen miles astern of *La Vaillante* at 6 o'clock in the morning. He described how Lieutenant Laporte, seeing the enemy gaining on him, ordered the ship's boats to be thrown over the side, followed by the oven and two anchors, as well as wetting the sails 'and doing everything possible to increase the speed of the ship'.

By nightfall, Perrier said, the enemy ship was not more than six miles astern and 'the captain ordered general quarters'. The wind was still very light and by 2 o'clock in the morning the enemy ship was within range. At daylight the enemy hoisted his colours and fired two broadsides 'which did much damage'. Perrier was not exaggerating: two broadsides from the *Indefatigable* – a cut-down ship of the line and carrying 44 guns – could be almost devastating for a small ship like *La Vaillante*.

Lieutenant Laporte 'then raised the national flag and ordered our guns to open fire. After a little time the enemy fired several broadsides to which we replied, but the enemy, a *rasée* frigate, was too strong for us to continue the battle, and this no doubt decided the captain to lower the flag at 5 o'clock on the morning of 21 Thermidor.'

The other man to give evidence was the second gunner, François Huguenin, a thirty-five-year-old corporal in the 5th brigade of Marine Artillery. His evidence was similar to Perrier's, except that he was able to give courses and wind directions, which Perrier had not noticed in the excitement. Huguenin described how every stitch of canvas was set on board *La Vaillante*, but even with the studdingsails drawing in the light wind the enemy gained on them. He described how the boat was slung over the side, the oven was demolished and thrown into the sea, and the anchors cut adrift. The enemy's first broadside, he said, cut the mizenboom topping-lift. And although *La Vaillante* managed to fire her starboard quarter guns at the enemy frigate, the salvoes 'were returned with many broadsides'.

Having heard all the witnesses and Laporte's own story, the court then considered its verdict and recorded that:

1. The court unanimously agreed that the corvette *La Vaillante* was taken on 21 Thermidor year 6 at 5 o'clock in the morning.
2. It is unanimously agreed that Citizen Pierre Laporte is not guilty of incapacity or negligence leading to the capture of *La Vaillante*, having from the moment he sighted the enemy warship done all that an experienced officer was able in such a case.

The president of the court then declared: 'The citizen Pierre Laporte is cleared of the charges against him.'

So Laporte returned to Bayonne, *La Vaillante*'s exchanged seamen were sent to other ships, the *déportés* in England set about trying to get used to a different way of life, and the priests settled down in their Dorset monastery, thankful not to be incarcerated at Cayenne.

While Proby and the *Danae* were in Plymouth for the repairs to his topmasts, he wrote an affectionate letter to his sister, Lady Charlotte Proby, on 21 January.

'My dear Charlotte,' he wrote from his cramped cabin,

I am afraid, by my not receiving an answer, that the letter I wrote to announce my arrival in port, has been sent on to my father in Ireland. I very stupidly directed it to him, to save the postage, without recollecting that it would go on a wild goose chase for a fortnight or three weeks before it would reach the proper hands.

You must HURRY and BUSTLE about most furiously to get a letter written that will reach me before I sail, for the ship has been ready these six days and I am in real expectation of orders.

The cocks and hens and rabbits and turkeys [at Elton Hall] must be left to themselves for one day as I am as arbitrary as Bonaparte, and I insist upon a joint letter [i.e. also from his other sister] immediately.

I have been trying to bribe the dockyard men here to let me cut off the head of one of the French prizes and stick it upon the *Danae*; it is the very image of Fanny, they have even painted her cheeks rosy, so alike that I could almost swear it was copied from the original. Your affectionate brother, Proby.

Just six days later, before Charlotte's reply could reach him, Proby sailed from Plymouth, bound once again for the Brittany coast. On 6 February, the *Danae* found herself in her only frigate action – although it was a one-sided affair.

The *Danae* had been in company with the 46-gun frigate *La Loire*, commanded by Captain James Newman, the 16-gun *Fairy*, Lieutenant J. S. Horton, the 18-gun *Harpy*, whose commanding officer, Lieutenant H. Bazely, Proby knew from previous operations together, and the 20-gun *Railleur*, commanded by Captain W. J. Turquand. It was ironic that three of the five British ships chasing the French frigate, the 40-gun *La Pallas*, were in fact French-built and taken as prizes – *La Loire*, the *Danae* and the *Railleur*.

It was not an exciting fight, since *La Pallas* had already been crippled during the night by the *Fairy* and the *Harpy* before *La Loire*, *Danae* and *Railleur* arrived on the scene. No sooner had *La Pallas* struck than Captain Newman, the senior officer present, divided up the French prisoners among the British ships present. Proby was far from pleased at finding he now had thirty-seven French prisoners on board, with orders to take them into Plymouth. Not only that, but Captain Newman took fifteen Danaes, several of them prime men, to help as prize crew on board the *Pallas*, so not only did Proby suddenly find his ship's company outnumbering the prisoners by a little more than three to one, but he had lost one of his two master's mates, one of three midshipmen, five able seamen, three ordinary seamen and five landsmen. It seems likely that Captain Newman quite ruthlessly formed *La Pallas*'s prize crew from men taken from his consorts, rather than using men from his own ship.

However, Proby was not far off Plymouth when he met the *Sophie* sloop, whose captain was junior to him. Lieutenant George Burdet was ordered across to the *Danae* and given written instructions while the thirty-seven French prisoners were ferried across in the *Danae*'s boats. Proby told Burdet in writing:

You are hereby required and directed to take on board thirty-seven French prisoners from his Majesty's ship under my command, and land them as soon as possible at Plymouth, after which you will continue to put into execution the orders you have received from Admiral Milbanke.

Proby, however, seems to have been doubtful about his action, and he wrote to the Admiralty saying:

I enclose herewith a copy of the orders I have given Captain Burdet of his Majesty's sloop *Sophie*. I hope their Lordships will approve of them; since the Start [Start Point] is in sight, she cannot be kept more than four and twenty hours off her station and the *Danae* is so short of complement that these prisoners in case of meeting a ship of equal force might be very troublesome, and they have already made the ship sickly.

I spoke a cartel yesterday from St Malo, the master of which informed me that the morning after the capture of *La Pallas* a man o' war brig and eight sail of storeships sailed from Brest. The wind, which continued strong from the SE, after my receiving Captain Newman's order, prevented my getting inshore before yesterday so that I am afraid the abovementioned convoy have arrived safe.

The French prisoners from *La Pallas*, once they arrived in Plymouth, were taken either to Mill prison or to the prison ships moored up the river. These were hulks, stripped of masts and yards, the gunports secured shut, and used as accommodation for prisoners and their guards. Conditions in the prison hulks were appalling, but until proper prisons were built – the great stone one at Princeton, on Dartmoor, is an example – there was little choice.

Officer prisoners were, however, frequently released on parole. In return for their word of honour that they would not escape, they were released and, providing they had enough money to pay for their lodgings, lived in private houses. Some of them used ivory, bone and wood to make ship models of extraordinary beauty, with all the details correct, and which they would then sell to help pay for their lodgings.*

Although Lieutenant Burdet of the *Sophie* sloop may have cursed at receiving thirty-seven Frenchmen and orders to take them into Plymouth, Proby had (as he mentioned in his letter to the Admiralty) just received orders from Captain Newman which 'prevented him getting inshore' to intercept the St Malo convoy. Whether to explain why he had missed the convoy or to criticize Captain Newman obliquely, Proby sent a copy of Newman's orders to the Admiralty:

> Having ordered Captain Turquand of his Majesty's sloop *Railleur* to put himself under [Proby's] command and follow your orders for his further proceedings, you are hereby required and directed to take him and the said sloop under your command accordingly, and use every exertion in your power to put the orders I received from the Right Honourable the Lords Commissioners of the Admiralty in execution, a copy of which you have enclosed, together with a copy of the intelligence communicated by Captain Lane.
>
> You are to continue on the above mentioned service until you receive further orders, transmitting to the Secretary of the Admiralty by every opportunity an account of your proceedings together with such intelligence as you may gain, proper to their Lordships' knowledge.

---

* The model-making skills of some of the prisoners, considering they had few if any tools and had to rely on their memories for details of the ships, are such that in the twentieth century the models are of considerable value, many of them being prized museum specimens.

## CHAPTER EIGHT

# THE DANAE'S
# LAST MUSTER

*P*roby's desperate and continuing shortage of men led him to press from any British privateers he could find. Privateersmen, by the very nature of the work, were probably the toughest and most ruthless men at sea. A privateer was a privately owned vessel whose owner had obtained a letter of marque (or commission) allowing him to operate against the enemy. He had to pay for any damage to his ship, but he took any enemy ship he captured into port and applied to the Admiralty court to have her declared a prize.

Once this happened and the captured ship was put up for sale, the privateer owner, master and crew divided all the proceeds on an agreed scale. This payment-by-results system meant that privateersmen fought desperately to make a capture, but they lived with the knowledge that the French were not their only enemy. Having a letter of marque gave the privateersmen no protection against being pressed into service by the Royal Navy. If a ship of the Royal Navy could force a privateer to heave to so that a lieutenant and some seamen could be sent on board, then most of the privateersmen could expect to be pressed: by law the Royal Navy had to leave on board only enough men to navigate the ship into the nearest friendly port.

There was, therefore, little love lost between the Royal Navy and privateers: most Royal Navy captains had a very poor opinion of privateers, regarding them as little better than pirates, and many admirals, Lord Nelson among them, considered that privateering should be stopped.

In late November the *Danae* had been within sight of a transport off Jersey when the ship signalled that she wanted to communicate with the British frigate. Proby sent over Lieutenant Rollo to see if he could press anyone and in the meantime the transport's captain came on board, complaining to Proby about the mutinous behaviour of a seaman called John McDonald, and 'begging I would take him out of his ship'. Proby agreed and the clerk, Giles, noted down McDonald's details – he had agreed to take the bounty, so was put down as 'vol', and he was rated an able seaman and made a foretopman, an indication that he was a trained and agile seaman whose job would be handling the topsail and topgallant on the foremast.

A ship's muster roll is in effect the accounts book, showing how many men are on board and their ratings, as well as their origins and, if they left the ship, where they went. The ship's company was mustered every seven or eight days. Mustering was in fact a roll call of every man in the ship, including the sick. Those on watch who could not be present to answer their names were 'checqued', which was then the Navy's way of writing 'checked'. The *Danae*'s ship's company was mustered four times in January and four times in February – the 7th, 14th, 22nd and 28th. The muster on the 28th was the last ever to be held on board the ship and gives a good opportunity to have a look at the ship's company.

It will be remembered that the *Danae* had an official complement of 155: that was how many men she *should* have carried. More important was the number listed in the muster roll as 'borne' – 116. So Proby at the end of February 1800 was short of thirty-nine men – a quarter of his official complement. Much worse was the fact that every time he captured a prize he had to give up more of his men as prize crew, and he would be lucky if he got them back. So every prize cost him a dozen or more men, and he had to rely on making up for men lost as prize crew by pressing more from privateers or merchant ships – not that he often found British merchant ships in the waters in which he cruised.

Of the 116 borne, eighty-nine men were actually mustered, answering when their names were called out, and twenty-five were 'checqued', and there were two sick. Of the nineteen Marines borne, fifteen were mustered and four (on sentry duty throughout the ship – at the waterbutt, the door to the captain's cabin, the magazine and the forehatch) were checqued.

Among the 116 names on the muster roll, it is worth noting a few. The most important is that of the twenty-four-year-old volunteer from Liverpool, William Jackson, mentioned earlier. Although he could neither read nor write, Jackson had an active brain; revolutionary thoughts were often in his mind, even though he had been in the *Danae* since July 1799, and had never been hauled before Lord Proby for insubordination or drunkenness. Jackson, for all that, was biding his time. John McDonald, only recently joined, had much in common with Jackson.

Six other names, listed one below the other, were of the five men from the *Bordelais* claiming to be Americans and one who said he was French. It will be remembered that three said they were from Virginia (John Brown III, James Brown II and Samuel Scarborough), David Greig claimed to be from Charleston, John Williams II from Boston (a man almost as important as Jackson) while Charles Goodrough was the Frenchman whose name was, in the coming weeks, to be spelled in a variety of ways.

Thus, apart from three shadowy figures yet to join the ship, all the actors in the forthcoming drama were present, and they included a man listed as Ignatius Fieney, aged twenty-four, rated an able seaman. The name below his is of an able seaman from Danzig, followed by a man from Hamburg. However, Fieney was an Irishman and a former priest 'and a lieutenant in the rebel army', according to evidence the first lieutenant gave later to a court martial.

The officers, warrant officers and Marines do not have their places of origin listed in the 'Where from' column of the muster roll, but the petty officers and seamen come from fifteen different countries. As the Irish were regarded as men of potentially doubtful loyalty (a charge not borne out by events) it is interesting to note the origins of the 108 men whose details are listed.

Fifty-one of the men and boys came from places in England, with no one county predominating. Twenty-four men came from Ireland, with the actual town or county rarely given. Six came from Wales and five from Scotland, while six men came from the Channel Islands. Of the foreigners, seven came (or claimed to) from America. And then one each gave as his place of origin Canada, Sweden, Newfoundland, Spain, Danzig, Hamburg, Madeira, Prussia and France.

The *Danae* was not unusual in the cosmopolitan nature of her ship's company; in fact the only unusual aspect is that she had hardly any Scandinavians on board. The reason for the variety of nationalities is easily explained: first, in a war affecting all of Europe, there was considerable unemployment everywhere, and those countries with big ports now found that the war had cut down drastically the amount of goods to be shipped – a port like Genoa, for example, which in peacetime supplied many ships and seamen, now found itself incorporated into France as the Ligurian Republic and with few cargoes and most of its ships laid up. So its seamen, unless they were to starve, had to sign on in whatever ships still went to sea, and these were mostly British.

Second, when seafaring was in a man's blood it was, if he came from a neutral country, of little consequence under which flag he sailed. A six-month voyage lasts six months whether under the American, British or French flag, and the country paying the best was usually chosen. The only risk for a seaman was in being impressed by one or other of the countries at war.

Where a neutral subject had been impressed by the Royal Navy it often seemed to the man worth taking the bounty and being listed as a volunteer rather than try to get released: unless he was an American with a Protection and had access to an American consul, the fact is that if he found himself in a British man o' war he was there until the war ended or he risked deserting.

At the end of February the *Danae* was back in Plymouth for provisions and Proby was preparing her to sail on what was to be her last voyage under the British flag. Amid the bustle of getting on board provisions and water, and receiving fresh beef from one of the port boats two or three times a week, there was the usual correspondence with the Admiralty. Proby had written to the Admiralty about the men he had lent to the *Pallas* prize, and Nepean answered: 'I have received your letter of the 1st' (Nepean was writing on the 3rd). Even allowing that Proby was using nautical time and Nepean civil, the letter took only two days to reach London. However, Proby never received Nepean's reply: the *Danae* sailed from Plymouth on 2 March, bound back to the Brittany coast with orders to cruise off Ushant.

On 10 March a sail was sighted and the *Danae* set off in chase, finding a captured British ship, the *Plenty*, with a French prize crew on board who were heading for Brest and intending to hand over the ship and the British prisoners to the French authorities. The *Plenty* was captured, and as soon as Proby had discovered what had happened he took the five Frenchmen of the prize crew on board the *Danae* as prisoners and sent the *Plenty* back to England with her original crew, who had still been on board her as prisoners.

The names of the five Frenchmen appear only once in all the documents relating to the *Danae* – on the list of payments of rewards by the French government. Listed separately (with the rest noted as 'foreigners') are Jean-Marie Cochet, Jacques Arondel, Jacques le Breton, Jean Voisin and Jean Anger.

No sooner had the *Plenty* been sent off to England and the five French prisoners – originally from the crew of the French privateer *Le Malouin*, which had captured the *Plenty* in the first place – secured than a period of settled weather made sailing a great deal easier, and Proby decided it was a good time to patrol through the Chenal du Four between Ushant and the mainland. However, the light winds and strong currents made it difficult to navigate along the coast – it was a matter of waiting for the current to turn fair and making a dash, hoping to be able to anchor in a sheltered place before current (or tidal stream) turned foul again, using the light wind to manoeuvre at slack water.

As far as all the officers and warrant officers on board the *Danae* were concerned, it was an ordinary afternoon, the only unusual thing being that for once it was not blowing half a gale of wind. The new master-at-arms, William White, noticed nothing out of the way when he made his rounds of the ship; the first lieutenant, Charles James Niven, saw nothing unusual. Nor did the chaplain, Thomas Allsop, notice any men muttering in groups.

The surgeon, Thomas Hendry, did not have an unusual number of men reporting sick nor did he notice any strange behaviour among the men. Thomas Mills, purser, Archibald Herron, midshipman and acting master's mate, John Hollowood, boatswain, the Hon. James Rollo, second lieutenant, and Robert Stevens, lieutenant of Marines – none of these men noticed anything unusual going on among the ship's company.

Yet thirty-eight seamen were about to mutiny, led by William

Jackson, the twenty-four-year-old seaman from Liverpool (who was later to claim that he was an American), and helped by John McDonald, the able seaman the master of the transport had begged Proby to take away, Ignatius Fieney, the Irishman and former priest, and John Williams II, the twenty-nine-year-old able seaman who was one of the men taken from the privateer *Bordelais*.

One thing seems certain: that the five French prisoners taken from the *Plenty* and who came from the privateer *Le Malouin* had nothing to do with the planning. They were being guarded by Lieutenant Stevens's Marines, and there is no way that Jackson, McDonald, Williams or Fieney could have spoken to them. More important, when some of the mutineers were later court-martialled, neither they nor the officers and seamen giving evidence against them, ever mentioned – except once in passing – the five Frenchmen.

In the morning there had been a flogging. On the previous day one of the boatswain's mates had made a new cat-o'-nine-tails, covered the handle with red baize, and given it to the boatswain to keep until it was needed.

At the time Proby had set for the flogging, a hatchway grating was set up vertically, all the officers assembled aft of it and the ship's company forward. The man, William Jeffereys, a thirty-two-year-old carpenter's mate from Penryn, in Cornwall, was brought up on deck, his shirt stripped off and a leather apron tied round his lower back, so that it protected his kidneys. Proby then stepped forward, said loudly what Jeffereys was charged with and then read out the particular Article of War covering the charge. He announced how many lashes Jeffereys was to be given, and said: 'Seize him up!'

The carpenter's mate was then secured with lashings by the arms and legs, spreadeagled and facing the grating. At a word from Proby one of the boatswain's mates took the cat-o'-nine-tails and gave Jeffereys the lashes ordered, running the tails through his fingers after each stroke so that the tails did not become entangled.

As the *Danae*'s log and journal are missing for this period we do not know exactly how many lashes Jeffereys was given, but when the punishment was completed he was allowed to go to his hammock and excused duties for the rest of the day. As William

White, the *Danae*'s master-at-arms, was later to testify, Jeffereys 'said he was sore and could not get out of his hammock to do his duty'.

After the flogging the men were piped to dinner, a meal they had at noon, and Proby would have returned to his tiny cabin while the officers not on duty went down to the gunroom, with its headroom of 4 feet 6 inches. The gunroom was like a small hall off which the officers' cabins led. In the middle of the gunroom was a table with forms down the long sides. Here the officers had their meals and often sat when they were tired of their cabins, which would have been small enough in a normal frigate but in the *Danae* were little more than hen coops. The officers and men moved below in a perpetual stoop, heads bent like penitent monks going about their business.

At 2.30 pm the *Danae* was sailing south through the Chenal du Four, with the mainland on the larboard hand and the island of Ushant over on the starboard bow. As Mr Huntingdon, the master, recalled, there was a light breeze and it was hazy. Suddenly the lookout at the foretopmasthead gave a shout. It was a shout which was to have an enormous effect on the *Danae*'s future.

## CHAPTER NINE

# THE ORGANIZERS

The lookout at the foretopmast gave an excited hail because in the distance ahead he could see several ships at anchor in the Chenal du Four. It was easy enough to be sure thay were at anchor because they had no sails set. That, Proby could see, was hardly surprising because the wind was so light that clumsy, laden merchant ships – which these almost certainly were – would be unable to make any headway against wind and tide, and very sensibly they had anchored.

What little wind there was came from the north-east and Proby gave the order to rig out studdingsails, which were in effect extensions of the normal sails and which could make all possible use of the following wind. But the wind was so light that the *Danae* made little progress. The master with his telescope counted eighteen vessels at anchor and what seemed to be a brig of war.

By the time the ships had been in sight for half an hour, it was seen from the *Danae* that they were setting sail and soon they were all under way, heading southwards away from the frigate and towards Pointe St Mathieu, obviously trying to make Brest. It was equally obvious that they would never reach Pointe St Mathieu in this light wind, and that the *Danae* would never catch up with them. The moment the tide turned it would carry the French ships along at the same speed as the *Danae*, and the haze in the sky gave no promise of more wind.

At 5 pm the *Danae's* master, Huntingdon, noted that the 'Rock le Four', which gave the channel its name, was bearing east, putting the *Danae* offshore of the village of Argenton, a few miles short of the little port of Le Conquet. It was becoming very clear to Proby that he did not stand a chance of catching the convoy and in the meantime he was getting farther into the Chenal du Four so that when the tide began to ebb he would not be able to beat out against the light north-easterly wind to prevent himself being swept southwards on to the outlying reefs and rocks. He gave the order to get the studdingsails in and then gave up the chase, turning the *Danae* so that she sailed back along her wake out of the Chenal du Four and away from Brest.

William Jackson, who was captain of the maintop, and John Williams, the able seaman from the French privateer *Bordelais,* who claimed to come from Boston and was one of the *Danae's* quarter gunners, along with several other seamen, noticed that the ship was turning away and heading out to sea, and they did some quick thinking. Every mile the *Danae* sailed back took her further away from Brest. They were not concerned with the French convoy now that it had fulfilled its role of getting the *Danae* nearer to Brest than she had ever been before: what did concern them now was that Lord Proby had given the order for the ship to wear round and they were sailing away from the coast. Jackson could not risk doing anything at any distance from Brest because there were always several British ships of the blockading squadron and others cruising the coast, as the *Danae* was doing herself, and if he succeeded in seizing the ship there was always the chance, unless he was very close inshore, of being intercepted. And being intercepted meant only one thing – a noose round his neck as he was hanged from the yardarm of one of the King's ships.

It has been possible to build up a detailed picture of the mutiny, and also to identify the ringleaders, thanks to their boasts later to the French authorities and the court martial evidence of some of the loyalists. It seems that in the afternoon Jackson met some of his fellow conspirators up in the maintop and later managed to pass the word to the thirty or more of the ship's company who were likely to join a mutiny without telling any men who were loyal and might raise an alarm. He seems to have concentrated on his own watch.

There were ways, depending on the ability of the conspirators, to get likely men apart from the rest, and to persuade them to take some sort of oath. In the *Hermione* the fore and maintop were favourite places – men could be aloft without needing excuses and without being seen – and this is probably what happened in the

*Danae*. All of the leading conspirators were topmen, although topmen were of course the youngest, toughest and most skilled among the ship's seamen, and thus likely to be the most headstrong and easily persuaded.

At this time the *Danae* was still very short of men, so much so that Proby had ordered Lieutenant Niven to put the idlers and officers' servants into watches. An idler, despite his name, was simply a member of the ship's company who did not normally stand a watch – a day worker, in effect. Such men were cooks, surgeon's mates, the carpenter and his mates. One important reason for the shortage of men is shown in the *Danae*'s last muster roll, in the French archives at Brest. Against the names of fifteen men is 'lent 6 Feb' – the men who had been sent to the *Pallas* on the orders of Captain Newman of the *Loire*.

For a ship's company Proby had ninety-four officers, warrant and petty officers and seamen, twenty Marines and sixteen boys. Absent from the ship, sent off as prize crews, were twenty-three men. The total number of men on board split into five officers, four midshipmen, four warrant officers, eighty-one petty officers and seamen, twenty Marines and sixteen boys.

Proby's position in the *Danae* as he saw it on 13 March (since noon, by nautical time it had been 14 March) was that he was almost critically short of men, and several of the men he had were sullen and truculent. Not mutinous, though; the six men from the *Bordelais* had been watched closely by Lieutenant Niven, Lieutenant Rollo and the master, Huntingdon, and they seemed to be doing their work properly. Indeed, some of them had been made topmen, a fact which showed they were the most skilled seamen in the ship: working aloft on the topsail and topgallant yards meant men had to be alert and nimble, able to fight stubborn canvas after climbing the ratlines as fast as they could go and then making their way sideways out along the yards. Usually if they were furling sails the wind was blowing hard and there was a sea running so that the ship rolled heavily, with the masts gyrating like upside-down pendulums, trying to hurl the men off the yards with the momentum. And usually the canvas was wet and stiff, whipped by the wind, and fighting against being hauled to the yard and secured by gaskets. Should a few square feet of canvas escape seamen's clutching hands it would flog about, doing its best to hurl the men off the yard on to the deck scores of feet below. To fall from either the topsail or the topgallant yard meant death.

But Proby knew that his command of the ship was backed up by the Articles of War: he had officers and petty officers to enforce his orders; behind him was the whole weight of the Admiralty. He was in fact king of the little island represented by the *Danae*. He had more power over his seamen than His Majesty. Proby could order a man to be flogged, but the King could not. He could order a man to be tried by court martial on a charge for which death was the invariable penalty. He could send men aloft in conditions which meant they risked being killed.

The men in the *Danae* knew all about the *Hermione* affair, even though it had happened across the Atlantic: John Brown, who claimed to be an American from Virginia, also boasted to his friends that he had served in the *Hermione*.*

So the afternoon passed, evening became twilight, watches changed, lookouts came down from aloft and were posted round the ship (six of them: on each side there was one in the bow, a second amidships and a third aft, watching the quarter). The purser issued lanterns – he had to supply the candles – and the off duty watch turned in to their hammocks. There was a Marine sentry, William Coburn, at the scuttlebutt – the cask of fresh water – and another at the door to the magazine. Proby appears to have dispensed with the Marine sentry who should have stood at his door.

What happened next emerges from the evidence of many officers, petty officers and seamen at courts martial of men subsequently caught and brought to trial. Jackson had obtained a Bible from somewhere and he and Williams approached several selected men in the fore and maintop during the afternoon, when the topmen were frequently aloft and out of sight and sound of anyone on deck. Jackson had chosen his men carefully, explaining his intentions to less than half the men in the *Danae*, so that when he acted more than half the ship's company were sleeping

---

* There is no record of this John Brown in the *Hermione*'s ship's company at the time of the mutiny, but had he served in that ship almost certainly he would have changed his name because the Admiralty had posters up everywhere listing the names of the *Hermione* mutineers, who were still being caught, tried and hanged. See *The Black Ship* by Dudley Pope, London and New York, 1963.

peacefully in their hammocks. Proby's servant, Thomas Brown, a twenty-year-old ordinary seaman from Lathbridge in Dorset, testified that one of the former *Bordelais* men said later that they had taken an oath on the Bible in the foretop 'not to do any murder but only to take the ship'. Brown identified the man with the Bible as Williams.

Jackson knew exactly whom he needed and the job each had to carry out if his plan was to succeed. For a start, the men needed arms, but all the cutlasses, tomahawks, pistols and muskets were kept locked up in the arms chest when not in use and the arms chest was, unusually, on the larboard side of the quarterdeck, a dozen feet abaft the wheel and, one would have thought, under the eye of the officer of the deck.

It was more usual to keep the arms chest below, and Lord Proby later explained why he had given orders for it to be stowed above decks. 'When I first took command of the *Danae*,' he told a court, 'I was stationed on an enemy's coast where I frequently anchored during the night; and I then judged it convenient but necessary to keep the arms up on deck where they could be reached at a moment's warning, preferably to keeping them below, in a small ship when the want of room would have obliged me to lumber them with other stores. Another reason,' he added revealingly, 'was that though I hoped and trusted, those cursed principles which had lately disgraced the British Navy were totally forgotten,* yet there was still a possibility of their having only subsided, and in case of a mutiny, it was madness to place the arms in the very berths of the mutineers.'

Archibald Herron, a midshipman and acting master's mate, had no doubt how the mutineers obtained the arms: 'One gunner's mate, Barney McGuire, and two of the gunner's crew, Brown and Williams, who called themselves Americans, were mutineers and could have procured them for them.' McGuire was a thirty-five-year-old Dubliner, while Brown was the coloured seaman from the *Bordelais*, and Williams, also from the same privateer, had already been busy helping Jackson. The gunner's mate was one of the men who would know where the key of the arms chest was kept, and one can only conclude that the *Danae*'s gunner, Israel

---

* Proby was referring to the mutinies of the fleets at Spithead and the Nore.

---

Lewis, who was not on board at this time, had not left important keys in the cabins of the captain or first lieutenant.

Jackson, Williams, James Brown and John McDonald, the seaman brought on board from the transport only three weeks earlier, had completed their work by nightfall, and at 8 pm the master, Huntingdon, was noting that the light breezes continued and the visibility was still hazy. The weather, although he did not say so, was obviously set fair for a few days, with the wind from the north-east and little more than fitful. It was quiet on board the *Danae*; the sea was calm enough that the ship's hull did not creak as it worked in the troughs and crests. Now there was only the occasional thump which shook the masts and rigging as sails hanging limply like huge curtains suddenly filled and slatted in a puff of wind. It was a time when the men on deck noticed the downdraught from the mainsail; a chilly breeze which blew down their necks. Usually there was enough wind blowing horizontally across the ship to disguise the downdraught; only in light winds was it apparent.

## CHAPTER TEN

# 'THE SHIP'S OURS NOW!'

The ship was under topsails and topgallants and had just enough steerage way for the sea to chuckle at the bow as it curled away from the cutwater. The starboard watch was on deck and, if anyone wanted to make a guess, the French convoy was probably safely anchored for the night off the little port and village of Le Conquet, with the masters of the ships hoping that the next morning's breeze would carry them round Pointe St Mathieu and let them turn eastward into the last fifteen miles up the river to Brest itself.

At 8.30 pm William White made his rounds of the ship. He inspected between decks and the upperdeck and found all was well. White, a volunteer from Alton in Hampshire, had been in the ship a month more than two years and had just been promoted from boatswain's mate to master-at-arms, a job which meant he was the ship's policeman. He noticed nothing unusual: down below several men had already turned into their hammocks – once the lanthorns were put out there was little else to do – and as soon as he had completed his rounds (which he would repeat every half an hour) he reported to the officer of the deck, in this case John Huntingdon, the master.

On watch, apart from John Huntingdon, who had the entire responsibility of the ship while he was officer of the deck, were Archibald Herron, the midshipman who was acting as master's mate and had charge of the watch under Huntingdon, another midshipman, William Spencer (described as 'a little boy', who was indeed going to end up the night in tears), and the quartermaster, James Cochrane, who had been promoted from able seaman by Proby in the last six weeks.

The quartermaster's job was to make sure that the man at the wheel was steering the correct course and the sails were drawing properly: for instance, when steering to windward that the luffs of the sails did not flutter. The man actually at the wheel (there were usually two men in a strong wind) was an able seaman, John Fleming, a volunteer who had been in the ship three and a half months. Both these men had been approached by Jackson, Williams or McDonald.

There were six seamen on the quarterdeck who completed the watch. As soon as the watch had changed at 8 pm and the port watch had gone below, Herron had mustered the men, and those answering their names were, in several cases, a sorry crowd to be on the quarterdeck of one of the King's ships should she have to go into action. Because he was so desperately short of men Proby had, as described earlier, given orders that officer's servants and idlers should be put into watches, and the first lieutenant, Charles Niven, had done his best to divide them up evenly.

The boatswain's mate of the watch was John Hall, a well trained seaman, but the next man whose name was called was James Jones, from Delton in Huntingdonshire, who was the purser's steward and unlikely to have much fire in his belly. Joseph Harris was a topman but the next man who should have been on watch was William Jeffereys, from Penryn in Cornwall, the carpenter's mate, more skilled with a chisel than a cutlass and who was at this time below in his hammock, recovering from the flogging. The fifth man was a topman, Thomas Holmes, who would be spending his watch in the foretop. The sixth was a Marine, William Coburn, the sentry at the scuttlebutt, the cask of water from which the men could drink at set times during the day.

Herron continued reading names and, as he testified later, although 'all the foretopmen answered, some of the maintopmen did not answer. Their names were Jackson and Nicholls . . .' Jackson was of course William Jackson, while the other man was Richard Nicholls, an ordinary seaman from Tonnerick, in Cornwall, who had been serving in the ship for fifteen months. Herron knew that Harris, one of the two other men who did not answer their names, was below in his hammock, on the sick list.

For reasons far from clear, when Herron reported to Huntingdon that he had mustered the watch, he did not report that several men had not answered their names, although it is unlikely that Huntingdon, who was to prove himself a dull-witted man, would have done anything about it. So the starboard watch took over on deck and Huntingdon gave the necessary helm orders to the quartermaster, James Cochrane. The only light on the quarterdeck came not from a guttering candle in the binnacle, giving a faint yellow glow over the compass, but from what Herron described as a 'patent oil lamp'.

At 9 pm the master-at-arms made his rounds again. Down below White saw Jeffereys lying in his hammock, his back cut from the flogging, but otherwise everything seemed normal: dozens of men were in their hammocks. After reporting once again to Huntingdon, he walked forward and sat down on deck between the fore and main hatchways, staying there until it was time to start his next half-hourly inspection of the ship. He neither saw nor heard anything to make him suspicious.

At that time the ship was quiet. Half the gratings were across the fore and main hatchways: the surgeon, Thomas Hendry, had requested this some weeks earlier, probably to keep the draught below from being too strong. There were three hatchways in the ship, with ladders giving the only means of going below or getting up on deck. Each hatchway could be closed by putting two gratings across, one on the fore side and one aft, closing off the ladder. These were heavy gratings, and in the case of the fore, main and after hatchways the half gratings on the forward sides were across, so that anyone wishing to go below or get up on deck used the ladder at the after end of the hatch. It had not escaped Jackson's attention that, because of the *Danae*'s flush deck design, if all three hatchways were shut with the gratings and secured, everyone below would be trapped.

As White was finishing his rounds just before 9.30 pm, Lord Proby was preparing to go to bed. The first lieutenant, Charles Niven was also just going to bed in his tiny cabin off the gunroom while Midshipman Waddy was in his hammock in the midshipmen's berth and Davis, the carpenter, was also in bed. Rollo, the second lieutenant, and the surgeon, Hendry, were still in the tiny gunroom. The purser, Mills, was in bed in his cabin and so was Lieutenant Stevens, the Marine officer. Some forty seamen and petty officers were in their hammocks below decks.

On deck, the master-at-arms made his usual report to Hunting-don. Only one thing had happened in the last half an hour, and White did not bother to report it: when he had been sitting between the hatches a seaman jumped below. 'I asked who it was,' White said later, 'and he said "It's me," but I do not know who it was.' After White had made his report, Huntingdon walked forward along the starboard side, and a minute later Herron followed him, passing the gunroom skylight. It was very dark; the haze cut down the starlight and the patent oil lamp illuminating the binnacle was not very strong, so that it should not dazzle the man at the wheel or the quartermaster.

Huntingdon suddenly found himself seized by four or five men and hustled forward along the deck. Huntingdon claimed later, 'I called out loudly for help, to make as much noise as I could, that the officers might hear below, but no one appeared.' Herron, a short distance behind him, gives a different and more likely account. It all happened, Herron said, when he was

walking the starboard side of the quarterdeck, opposite the gunroom skylight, the master walking the same side abreast of the after hatchway [and] four or five men (Jackson was one; I do not know the others) came and pushed and forced the master forward to the gangway when many others, upwards of a dozen of them, seized the master and struck him with their cutlasses, at the same time he hollering out loudly, 'What, what is the matter? What does all this mean?' He sung out, 'Help, help, what do all this mean?'

I was going fast to Mr Huntingdon's assistance when I was stopped by fourteen or fifteen armed men with cutlasses in their hands and pistols at their waists, crying 'Down with you, down with you, or we'll knock your damned head off, the ship's ours now, and we are now masters!'

Then I looked round to see if there were any on deck but mutineers. I saw none that offered to come to my assistance, the people still threatening me with the same words and cutlasses brandishing over my head. I going to the after hatchway with reluctance, seeing there could be nothing done.

Lord Proby came running up the after hatchway. He got within one step of the top of the ladder when one of them, I think it was Brown, a black man, but I am not positive, struck him with a cutlass on the head (he had no hat on) and down the captain tumbled to the foot of the ladder. They then pushed me down with their cutlasses. At that moment they dropped the grating on the after part of the hatchway, the other [part] was on before.

Huntingdon had in the meantime been forced down the hatchway. 'I called out loudly to give the alarm,' he said later, but 'they cut me over the head and struck me in different places . . . Being stunned with the cuts and blows I had received in the head, I was a little while senseless.'

Down below, the first person to raise the alarm had been the Marine officer, Lieutenant Stevens. Lord Proby described his role later:

As the Marine officer was in a cabin near the after hatchway he tried to get up on deck, but was thrown back before he ran to inform me.

I immediately attempted to force [my way] up but I was soon wounded and knocked down. When I collected myself again I found there was no chance but in the officers being able to get their arms and give me their joint support before the grating could be put on, and with that intention I ran aft for my sword but it was scarcely out of its scabbard when Lieutenant Niven came in to inform me that every grating in the ship was down, and upon examining to find if there was any means of forcing them, it appeared that the booms were cut down on the fore and main hatchways and the after one was secured with shot and capstan bars.

With mutineers now guarding every hatchway and Huntingdon and Herron bundled below, they now had complete control of the ship. Both the quartermaster, Cochrane, and Fleming, the man at the wheel, were mutineers, and not one man on deck went to help Huntingdon and Herron. Not every man on deck and in the tops, however, was a mutineer. Thomas Holmes, for instance, was a topman and he had been sitting in the foretop at the beginning of his watch when he 'heard a great noise. I got up and looked over the top rail and saw cutlasses rattling about. I thought they were going to quarters, and made all the haste I could.'

His station for general quarters was down on deck so he scrambled down the ratlines. 'I saw John Elliot, the captain of the fo'c'sle there. I asked him, "What is the matter, is there a sail in sight Johnny?"

'He said no, it was a mutiny. He told me that if I could get down below I had better get out of the way. I got down below and saw two men standing sentry over the fore hatchway, and a great many aft. I took and jumped down the fore hatchway ladder and went aft to my officer.'

Between the gunroom and Lord Proby's cabin there was a good deal of confusion. To begin with both Proby and Huntingdon were in Proby's cabin, both bleeding badly from head wounds, and a dazed Proby tried to work out what to do next, realizing that the mutineers now controlled the ship and, with the gratings across the hatchways, all the officers and loyal men were trapped below.

Lieutenant Niven described how he was called and after getting a dirk 'ran in my shirt to the after hatchway', where he met Lord Proby, wounded. He saw several cutlass blades sticking down through the holes in the grating.

The officer of Marines and, I think, the carpenter, reported the fore and main hatchways to be also secured. I then went to Lord Proby's cabin and found him bleeding from some cuts he had received on his head, and the master in the same situation.

I then received Lord Proby's orders to cut down the hammocks and take the names of the men below. His Lordship also desired me to order the officer of Marines to collect his party and arm them with such arms as we could find. I complied with these orders.

While the blood was being wiped off both the captain and master, seamen were arriving at the gunroom door – the gunroom was one of the few places where there was a lantern – to report.

One of the first men to report his name was John Hall, who had been bosun's mate of the watch and the first to answer when Herron mustered the watch. He said later that he had been going

aft along the deck with a lanthorn when William Jackson met him
with a cutlass in his hand, and John McDonald, the captain of the
foretop, took the lanthorn out of his hand.

I asked them what they were about. They told me they meant to
take the ship into France [and] asked me if I would join them,
and I told them no, I would not wish to have any hand in it but I
would rather go out of the way.
I went to the fore hatchway and they had got one grating on.
At the time they were looking for the other I got below. The
sentry who was standing there [who saw] me after I got down
asked who that was and I told him it was Hall. He then told me to
hand up some lanthorns and candles. I told him I was not the man
to apply to for them, he must go to the purser's steward for them.

Hall was not being obstructive: supplying lanthorns and candles
was the responsibility (and expense) of the purser, and the man
who actually gave them out (and collected them next morning) was
James Jones, the purser's steward, one of the men mustered on the
quarterdeck earlier in the evening by Herron.
'I then left the hatchway,' Hall concluded, 'and went aft. The
hatchways were all secured down then. I gave my name in to the
officer and was desired to stay aft in case there should be any
likelihood of taking the ship back.'
In fact the purser's steward had been very close to Hall at the
time of his conversation with the sentry. Jones told how:

I was looking down upon the lee gangway on the larboard side
about twenty minutes after nine. I heard a noise on the starboard
side of the quarterdeck. I thought it was the hands doing their
duty till a light from one of the cabins below shone up the after
hatchway. I saw a number of men armed with cutlasses and
pistols. They drove Mr Herron, the mate, off the deck and black
Brown called for Edwards, one of the carpenter's crew and a
mutineer, to come and lay the after grating on. Jackson said, 'We
have got the ship now in our possession and we will take her in to
France. The first man who attempts to come up the hatchway I'll
blow his brains out.'
I then went to the main hatchway and the grating next the

cable [i.e. the forward one] was just on. I went below and went
to the cabin to the officers where I saw the captain and master
both wounded. I gave my name in and went forward to the
gunner's store room, and going by the fore hatchway they fired a
pistol down between decks. I went into the store room to look
for arms to stand in our defence against the mutineers if they
should attempt [sic] but they had got them all on deck.

Another of the men giving his name to the officers was William
Jeffereys, who was recovering from his flogging. He testified:

I was in my hammock asleep. The first man I spoke to was John
Hall after he jumped down from the deck. I asked him what was
going on on deck. After once or twice asking him he told me
there was a mutiny.
   Then I saw the second lieutenant going between decks to see
how many people were below to order them aft. I immediately
got up and put on a pair of drawers and my jacket and went into
the gunroom and gave my name in. From that I went into the
cabin to see if any of my help should be wanted and was ready to
assist in anything the officers should request.

It should be noted that in a frigate there was only one 'cabin',
which was the captain's cabin and which in a larger frigate was
divided into 'the coach' or day cabin, and a sleeping cabin, and in
big vessels, a dining cabin.
   Thomas Holmes, who had been in the foretop, jumped down
the fore hatchway ladder and went aft to his officer. 'The lieutenant
said "Who is this?" I said "Holmes." He said, "Stay aft, Holmes."
I said, "Very well." He gave me a knife to cut down the hammocks
all on one side. I did so and then went aft again.'
   Proby had given Lieutenant Niven the order to cut down all the
hammocks below because apart from making it easier to see
through the ship it made sure that no mutineers, or potential
mutineers, were hiding below among the forty-odd seamen who
had been sleeping when the mutiny started.
   Proby also ordered all the cabins and store rooms to be searched
for arms. The search resulted in the discovery of ten cutlasses, four
muskets 'and some pocket pistols,' Proby wrote later, 'which were

distributed to the most trustworthy of almost forty men who were asleep in their hammocks when the affair took place.'

Many of the sleeping men had been Marines and typical of them was Private Lawrence Dowling, who later described his experiences. He had been in his hammock when the corporal of Marines, William McNulty,

came to my hammock and begged me for God's sake to turn out, or words to that purport, if I had a mind to save my life. On which I turned out immediately, thinking the ship was on the rocks.

As soon as I slipped on my jacket and trousers I ran directly to the after hatchway, thinking to go on deck. One of the men who was sentinel over the hatchway made a blow at me with a cutlass, on which I stepped back and saw [John Marret, an able seaman from Jersey] with a cutlass and pistol.

I inquired of [another] sentry who guarded the hatchway what was the matter. He replied, 'You had better go about your business. You shall know presently,' or words to that effect. Directly after that they laid over the gratings and the tarpaulin.

What Private Dowling thought was a tarpaulin was in fact the mizen staysail, which was dragged over the booms and held down with handspikes and piles of shot to prevent any of the prisoners below from looking up and perhaps recognizing individual mutineers. The sentry who sent Dowling about his business was William Moreland, a twenty-one-year-old landsman from County Down. This young Irishman had been serving in the *Danae* for three months short of two years and was the gun-room cook.

Once the gratings were down, the mutineers had little more to do to secure the upperdeck: all the mutineers were up there and the loyal men were trapped below. Four men seem to have been giving all the orders – William Jackson, two men from the *Bordelais*, Williams and Brown III, the black man, and John McDonald, the new seaman from the transport. Lord Proby's impression, however, was that William Jackson and John McDonald 'appeared to command the ship alternately'.

With the wind so light it did not matter that Jackson could not spare much time to give helm orders, but Cochrane, the quarter-master, continued to keep the sails filled.

One of the most pathetic figures on deck was the 'little boy', Midshipman William Spencer, who was bewildered by the suddenness with which the mutineers had seized Huntingdon and Herron, his two superiors on the quarterdeck. When asked later: 'Were you kept upon deck by the mutineers, or did you stay there of your own choice?' he admitted quite frankly, 'I stayed there on my own choice because I did not know where I was safest.'

He ended up in the galley (which was on deck forward) with the ship's cook and the Marine who had been sentry at the scuttlebutt and firmly refused to join the mutiny, Private Coburn. Because the gratings were down by the time they came to deal with Coburn, the mutineers confined him in the galley, where he was joined by Midshipman Spencer. Williams looked in later, still limping from an accident which had happened with a 6-pounder gun a couple of days earlier. At his trial, Williams, defending himself, asked the midshipman, 'Do you remember you was crying at the time?' at which Spencer said, 'Yes.'

The wind was so light there was no chance of steering the ship right through the Chenal du Four to Pointe St Mathieu, and for a while she was lying-to. But with so many excited men suddenly getting power, there was a good deal of shouting. Jackson posted lookouts round the ship, and down below Proby and the other officers frequently heard Jackson, McDonald, Williams and Brown calling out to the men to keep a sharp lookout. It was ironic that in a matter of minutes the situation had changed: until then the oft-repeated call to the lookouts had been to ensure that they kept a careful watch for French ships. Now the mutineers were warning their lookouts because of the risk of sighting another British ship.

It was now that the other active mutineers revealed themselves, and many months later various of the *Danae*'s officers and warrant officers were asked to name the ringleaders. Proby showed no hesitation: they were, he said, William Jackson, three men named Brown – John Brown I, the quarter gunner who came from Cumberland and had later claimed to have been in the *Hermione*; John Brown II, Lord Proby's coxswain; and John Brown III, a black seaman from the *Bordelais*; Charles Goodrough, from the *Bordelais*; Alexander Robertson, from Aberdeen, twenty-two years old and an able seaman; John McDonald; a man whose name he gave as Charles Lightoff but who was in the muster roll as Carl Leitoff, the twenty-seven-year-old from Danzig and an able seaman; James Cochrane, the forty-five-year-old Whitby man who had been promoted quartermaster less than six weeks before the mutiny and whose voice, Proby said, 'I could clearly distinguish'; and Ignatius Fieney.

William White, the master-at-arms, gave names of those he considered ringleaders and the reasons why. William Jackson,

from having heard him give orders when the ship was in the possession of the mutineers; Brown [I] one of the quarter gunners, from having boasted after the ship was in the possession of the French, that he had belonged to the *Hermione* and was saying something of the treatment of the officers; John Williams II from being one of the crew of the *Bordelais*, a French privateer taken by the *Révolutionnaire*; George Gardner from wearing the master's coat and boasting openly that he had cut the master's head; Thomas [sic: John] McDonald for giving orders while the ship was in their possession; William Cootes [sic: William Cotes, a volunteer and a twenty-two-year-old able seaman from Liverpool] . . . William Moreland for having hailed the French boats and called out '*Vive la République Française*': Brown the captain's coxswain who was exceedingly active in giving orders to the men at the wheel. Wright steered the ship.

The carpenter, Thomas Davis, named Jackson, Williams the quarter gunner, Brown the black man and Samuel Scarborough, yet another of the six men from the *Bordelais* who was a twenty-year-old ordinary seaman claiming to be from Virginia.

George Rogers, a master's mate, named William Jackson, the quarter gunner Brown I, the Scotsman Robertson named by Proby, and the black man, Brown III. The Marine lieutenant, Robert Stevens, picked out Jackson, Williams, McDonald and Brown III, while the second lieutenant, Rollo, named Jackson, McDonald and the quartermaster, Cochrane.

And there were those that became mutineers by mischance. Lieutenant Stevens told one case. 'There was a man, Jarvis, I think his name, who expressed sorrow [to me] in France, saying that if he had not been asleep on deck at the time he should not have known anything about it.' The man was one of the oldest of the ship's company, Thomas Jarvis, an ordinary seaman from Bristol and fifty-four years old. Having woken up among the mutineers he stayed with them.

Lord Proby described how things were going below. He had distributed the arms they had been able to find,

with an intention (as the wind would not then permit them to lay through the Passage [sic] du Four) of keeping them from the water and by that means forcing them to fight us upon fair terms.

About an hour after the mutineers got possession of the deck they put her head to the northward and I then proposed chocking the rudder, but at the same time laid before my officers my reasons for thinking it would be better to defer the execution for some time, and they agreed with me entirely.

Proby's reasons for chocking or wedging (so that the rudder could not turn) were:

First, as we were very far into the Passage, where they could always anchor and send ashore for troops, when they found themselves unable to manage the ship [because the rudder was chocked] without any likelihood of being molested by English cruisers, I thought it wiser to wait till she made some northing, but this plan was defeated by its being nearly calm and they lying-to till towards morning when the wind came more to the eastward and they made sail through the Passage.

Lieutenant Niven's version of the events was:

Lord Proby then proposed chocking the rudder and firing up the hatchways should we discover any number of mutineers together, but upon looking at the chart and getting a compass into the cabin, we supposed ourselves in the Passage du Four and Lord Proby said it was better to stand fast chocking the rudder until we were round St Matthews [Pointe St Mathieu] as we would then stand a chance of being picked up by our cruisers off the Black Rocks.

From our situation we all agreed with his Lordship that it was better to do so and Lord Proby desired me to knock out the bow scuttles on the larboard side and endeavour to make out what part of the Passage du Four we were near, which I did and reported to his Lordship 'Somewhere about Conquet.'

Proby did not abandon altogether the idea of chocking the rudder, which could be done from his cabin, through which the rudder post passed. The carpenter, Thomas Davies, worked out how best to do it, and one of his mates, William Jeffereys, his back still raw from the flogging, was 'very active' in bringing carpenter's tools aft ready to do the actual chocking, according to the first lieutenant.

The next thing Proby needed to know was the direction in which the mutineers were taking the ship, and Niven has already described his own role. Lord Proby testified:

I now ordered the scuttle to be knocked out forward, and a good lookout to be kept there and from the scuttle in the cabin with the intention as soon as she passed St Mathieu Point to chock the rudder; the mutineers would have been obliged either to give the ship up to the Brest [British] cruisers or to have fought the officers and loyalists.

Both alternatives were desperate for even if they succeeded in the latter case, their numbers would have been so weakened that they could not have worked the ship in a chase.

Having had the portholes knocked out so he could see where the ship was going, and work out her position by being able to see the coastline, did not help because, as Proby later said, 'I was here again defeated by the weather, for it fell calm about 11 a.m. and the mutineers anchored . . .'

William Jackson and his fellow mutineers had been carefully working the ship inshore and as soon as the wind had turned to the eastward they had been able to steer directly for Le Conquet, where they could soon see that the convoy and its escort were still lying at anchor under the guns of the fort, with the escorting corvette lying to seaward of them.

# CHAPTER ELEVEN

# SURRENDER
# AT LE CONQUET

While Jackson and McDonald worked the ship up towards Le Conquet, the officers below had been busy doing their best to see what was happening on deck, collecting information that was later to lead some mutineers to the noose. Lieutenant Niven told later how 'soon after it was daylight' he went to the after hatchway 'to endeavour to see the men upon deck. I found the after gratings secured with capstan bars, and a sail over the gratings, but a part of the gratings was not covered with the sail, and I saw [John Marret] through the part which was not covered.

'William Moreland stood upon the starboard side of the hatchway and [Marret] upon the larboard side armed with a pistol and a cutlass. I saw him also speaking to McDonald and John Brown III at the larboard gangway.'

The man at the wheel was Thomas Wright, a Scot from Chadborough, in East Lothian, a twenty-three-year-old seaman down in the muster roll as a volunteer.

Proby thought of appealing to the mutineers, pointing out that they were likely to be hanged if they were ever caught. He earlier decided to make them an offer – that he would take the ship to Plymouth and 'transmit to the Admiralty any complaint they might have to make of the officers' conduct'. He realized that he and his first lieutenant were unlikely to carry much weight with the mutineers, so he called the chaplain, Mr Thomas Allsop, and explained to him what he wanted the mutineers to hear.

Allsop went to the after hatchway and delivered the strangest sermon of his life through the grating to the men above him, but it had no effect. 'He was answered in a very insolent manner by Jackson and McDonald,' Lieutenant Niven commented later.

Proby's offer was one the mutineers had to reject out of hand because, once the ship was back in Plymouth, the authorities would regard them as the mutineers they were and arrest them immediately and put them on trial. But it was the only offer Proby could make.

As soon as it was seen that the ship was approaching Le Conquet, Proby collected up the secret books – *The Signal Book for Ships of War*, the private signals for a three-month period for the Channel Fleet, his journal which he had been keeping since New Year's Day, having sent the one for the previous three months to the Admiralty, and the master's log. They were all put into a canvas bag in which there was a large piece of lead and which had a lace-up neck. The Articles of War made very clear the severe penalties facing any captain who failed to prevent the secret papers falling into the enemy's hands, and Proby himself dropped them over the side through the after scuttle.

The only book that was not thrown into the sea was the muster roll, which must have been overlooked. It was later found by the French authorities and used by them as a checklist naming the men who had been on board (along with those who had been lent to other ships).

William Jackson, having got the *Danae* through the Chenal du Four and up to Le Conquet without apparently sending the French convoy scuttling or disturbing the escorting corvette *La Colombe*, then sailed close up to the fort beside the river forming the harbour.

The young midshipman, William Spencer, still wandering around the ship after spending a tearful night in the galley with the cook and the Marine, Private Coburn, then saw John Marret, the Channel Islander, hail the fort. 'To the best of my understanding, as he spoke French which I understood little,' Spencer said afterwards, 'he desired the French to send a party of troops on board.'

The fact that the convoy did not bolt and *La Colombe* did nothing is probably explained by the *Danae*'s origins. As she approached Le Conquet she was flying French colours above the British, and being French-built as a corvette, thus having a distinct shape, the same type of vessel as *La Colombe* herself in fact, the French almost certainly assumed from her appearance that she was

French. Otherwise she would never have got near the convoy without it bolting and certainly she would have been fired on by the fort long before she was close enough to hail.

The *Danae* then anchored. Lieutenant Niven said he had just returned to Captain Proby's cabin when 'I saw the jolly boat lowered from the stern, and heard afterwards several boats approaching the ship'.

Proby described the next few minutes, from 2 o'clock in the afternoon, in a letter to the Admiralty. 'A large detachment of French troops came on board and as there was no longer the most distant prospect of doing his country a service by further opposition, [Lord Proby] surrendered.'

Lieutenant Niven, watching from the scuttle aft, saw McDonald giving a rope to the French boats. Later he saw 'the people on the after part of the quarterdeck go forward and hoist the foretopsail in consequence of [McDonald's] orders, who had previously been spoken to by one of the French prisoners then upon deck'.

The arrival of the French troops created bedlam. None of the French soldiers spoke English, and the first story of what had happened on board the *Danae* came from the five former Malouins, John Marret – who, as a Channel Islander, was bilingual – and Charles Goodrough.

While explanations were going on, some of the mutineers started furling the *Danae*'s sails and there were sporadic outbursts of cheering. As soon as the French troops managed to understand exactly what had happened they decided to send all the loyalists on shore, the officers going first to the *Colombe*, whose captain had sent across the boarding party.

The *Danae*'s remaining boats were hoisted out and soon the ship's officers were mustered on deck and ordered down into one of them. At this point the Marine, Coburn, who had been sentry at the scuttlebutt but had resolutely refused to join the mutineers, came across the deck to join Lord Proby, declaring (according to Lieutenant Niven later) 'that the mutineers would not suffer him quit the deck before and that at the commencement of the mutiny he was afraid to quit his post as sentinel over the scuttlebutt.'

As the officers went down into the boat, they were careful to look round them. Lieutenant Niven said: 'When I was put in a boat after the ship had surrendered to the French troops, McDonald, one of the ringleaders, was abusing Lord Proby, which induced his Lordship and myself to look up to the gangway, where I saw [John Marret] just above us armed with a sword and pistol.' Lord Proby recalled that McDonald 'had a brace of pistols in his belt'.

Lieutenant Niven said later that he heard McDonald, when pointing to Lord Proby, 'make use of the words "*Noblie de Diable – noblie de merdo*" and, addressing himself to the Frenchmen, said Lord Proby gave six dozen [presumably lashes] for the royal bowlines and that it was him that cut them'. By this McDonald was apparently referring to an incident when the royal bowlines (ropes used to extend the sail) were wilfully cut and Lord Proby had ordered a flogging.

Marret and Niven were to meet later in strange circumstances that were to prove fatal for the seaman.

Lieutenant Rollo spotted another ringleader as he made his way down into the boat after Lord Proby and the other officers. Rollo saw John Williams, one of the men from the *Bordelais*, 'sitting on the hammock cloth just by the after hatchway' and looking over the side, watching what was going on. Williams's voice (recognized by several officers when they were below) and his curiosity were later to put him on trial for his life.

While some mutineers continued furling the sails, others manned the boats to row those carrying the officers to the *Colombe* and the rest of the loyal men to land at Le Conquet. As soon as they were on board the *Colombe*, Proby and his officers formally surrendered their swords to her captain. There was no dishonour in surrendering to the enemy but it was unthinkable to surrender to mutineers.

All the loyalist Danaes were housed for the night at Le Conquet – they had begun to be ferried on shore between three and four o'clock – while the mutineers were given orders to take the *Danae* round to Brest. In the meantime a messenger was sent to Brest to tell the authorities of the *Danae*'s arrival.

The French naval headquarters in Brest is a large building among circular towers in the walled dockyard and called the Château. In earlier days, prisoners of war were kept in the Château under grim conditions, but in 1779, twenty-one years before the *Danae*'s arrival, a new 1,600-bed hospital was planned to be built at

Pontanezen, a village to the north-east of Brest in open country.*
The hospital was never built but two years later the Navy bought
the land and put up three buildings. The first was to be used as a
hospital, the second for housing prisoners (naval in peacetime, and
enemy in time of war), and the third as a barracks. During the
present war, Pontanezen was used to house prisoners of war
temporarily until they acould be transferred to permanent prisons
in the interior, such as Valenciennes.

The administration in Brest was divided into civilian and naval.
The chief of administration of the Marine in Brest was Citizen
Moreau, who was *Préfet Maritime* of the third *arrondissement*.
The *Chef Militaire* was Rear Admiral Morard de Galle, who
commanded the large arsenal on both sides of the River Penfeld
which divides Brest. The ships in Brest were commanded by Rear
Admiral Eustache Bruix. They were further divided into the ships
which were in the harbour and on which the dockyards were
working, and which came under the *Commissaire Principal*, and
those in the Roads which were under the command of Rear
Admiral de Galle.

By far the busiest man, however, was the *Ordonnateur*, or *Chef
d'Administration*, who was Benoît Georges Najac, the director of
the port and responsible for ship construction and repairs, and
acting as paymaster and victualler as well as being responsible for
the hospitals and surgeons. In one or other of these roles, Najac
was to become responsible for all the Danaes, both loyalist and
mutineers.

*Ordonnateur* Najac had his office not in the Château, which
overlooks the harbour and roads, but in the Hôtel St Pierre on the
Rue de Siam, then the main street of Brest and on the road to Paris,
and almost a kilometre from the Château. The Hôtel St Pierre had
an interesting history: it was bought by the Marquise de Crève
Coeur in 1752 and served as accommodation for student officers
acting as guards of the flag admiral and marine guards. In 1771 it
was given to the *Préfet Maritime*† and it was to there that news

---

* But now a suburb of Brest. The barracks were used by American troops in the
First World War, and from May to November 1918, 810,000 American soldiers
stayed there before going on to the front.
† It remained the *Préfecture Maritime* until 1940. It was destroyed by American
forces during the liberation of Brest in 1944.

came of the sudden arrival of the *Danae* at Le Conquet. Najac at once gave orders for the loyalists to be marched from Le Conquet to Pontanezen while the ship herself was to be brought round to Brest – a short voyage southwards to round Pointe St Mathieu and then turn eastward up to Brest itself.

After the news had been sent to the Minister of Marine in Paris in a brief telegraphic message, *Ordonnateur* Najac immediately wrote a letter to the Minister:

> A frigate or large English corvette, called the *Danae*, carrying 22 [sic] guns of 32 pounds and with a crew of 110, surrendered yesterday without opening fire, because of a mutiny due to the intrepid temerity of five French sailors coming from a St Malo privateer.
>
> She was boarded by the corvette *La Colombe* and taken to Le Conquet, where I have just given orders for the disembarkation of prisoners.
>
> Immediately I have gathered further details of this truly astonishing prize I will hasten to transmit them to you.

The Minister of Marine immediately passed the news on to the First Consul and, as will be seen, Bonaparte's curiosity was aroused.

More than fifty officers, warrant officers, petty officers, seamen and Marines from the *Danae* started the long march from Le Conquet across the neck of Pointe St Mathieu on a road running parallel with the entrance to Brest. It passed through the villages of Le Trez-Hir and Plouzané (where there were batteries) and into the western side of the port. Finally it passed through the last western suburb, Kerangoff, before reaching the Penfeld River, which divides Brest, with the Château and Hôtel St Pierre on the eastern side. Well guarded, the prisoners trudged across the Pont Levant which leads directly to the Rue de Siam, so that the Danaes had to pass Najac's office in the Hôtel St Pierre on their way to Pontanezen.

In the meantime French officers and seamen from the *Colombe* had taken command of the frigate for the short voyage round to Brest roads. William Jackson gave the orders to the mutineers, with men like Marret and Goodrough acting as translators and the five French former prisoners from the *Plenty* at last free and among their own people.

As soon as the ship was brought into Brest and safely anchored, the mutineers were taken off to Pontanezen, where they were kept close to but separate from the loyalists and were not locked up. The loyalists had been preceded by an order sent by *Ordonnateur* Najac to the Commissioner of Hospitals at Brest: 'I beg you, Citizen, to give orders to have confined the captain, first lieutenant and crew of the English frigate the *Danae*, and to give orders that they have no communication with anyone except those going to Pontanezen for reasons proper and recognized by the service.'

With the mutineers off the ship, the French then searched it carefully and found the muster roll, with its note that the ship's company had been mustered four times in January and four times in February. There had been no muster in March, and one was overdue. Armed with the muster roll, listing every man who had been in the ship from Lord Proby to the youngest boy, 3rd class, the French authorities then began checking up exactly who they had. By sorting out both loyalists and mutineers at Pontanezen, they were able to mark up the muster roll. Against the name of every man who was in the roll but away from the ship on board a prize (many had not had the right column filled in because the muster was overdue) there was a dash. Against the name of each loyalist there was a tick. Every mutineer was marked with 'M' or 'Mut' except for one man. Against the name of William Jackson was written 'M.C.', presumably standing for *Mutin en Chef*. Only the three classes of boys, 1st, 2nd and 3rd class, and the Marines, had their names left unmarked. This was a strange omission because some of the boys and the Marines had joined the mutineers.

*Ordonnateur* Najac wrote to the Minister of Marine in Paris:

The port is busy with the inventory of the *Danae*. Four of the five French and three of the English who helped take the ship left here the day before yesterday for Paris by the order of the First Consul. I have paid each one a sum of 72 francs in addition to travelling expenses, clothing and food which I have provided. They travel under the guard of an officer of the Gendarmerie.

I have agreed to pay the same sum of 72 francs to all those who took part in the mutiny. They have testified their desire to return [sic] to Bordeaux to sail in merchant ships there. I have given them passports.

Najac also enclosed a copy of a tribunal's report on the taking of the *Danae*. He added that the prisoners of war from the *Danae* who were all at Pontanezen were going to be taken to Valenciennes, which was the main prison.

The *Danae* had not been at anchor long before Najac sent an inspector and some assistants on board to make the inventory of all the stores on board. They had a busy time knocking out bungs and sniffing or tasting the contents of barrels and making a list. It was a long job – a note at the bottom of the inventory says: 'The survey began the 15 Germinal [4 April] after midday at 2 o'clock and finished the 17th in the morning at 10 o'clock.'

There were two casks of Madeira, eight barrels of rum and fifteen barrels of brandy, ensuring that the officers had enough to drink with their meals and that there was sufficient liquor to issue the Danaes their daily tots. There was a barrel of vinegar and another of molasses. Cheese was a favourite food of the seamen (and a nickname for the purser was 'Nip Cheese'), and the *Danae* had fifteen barrels of it on board. The rest of the inventory was of staple items – flour, oatmeal, cocoa, butter, lard, salt beef, vegetables and eighty-five sacks of biscuit (which, used as bread, was a hard-baked disc unless age and weevils reduced it to crumbling softness).

*Ordonnateur* Najac in a letter of 11 April appointed a tribunal to investigate the mutiny and determine the mutineers' rights, to enable the authorities to decide on 'the validity and legality of the seizure'.

'In consequence,' says Najac's report of the tribunal, 'three men being part of the crew who mutinied, and the only ones found at this moment, have been informed and conducted to my presence in one of the offices of the Navy where, with the assistance of Citizen Langlohts, sworn and licensed interpreter, the said men were interrogated in the presence of Citizens Roustargneng, Controller of the Navy [in Brest], Davignon, principal officer of the Customs, and Berubé.'

The report noted: 'The importance of the objective required that the sailors be interrogated separately. I had warned them that they would be kept in the nearby room while one of them would answer the questions that would be put to him.'

The first of the three was brought in and asked his name, age, usual domicile and rank. He answered that his name was Domini-que Gunay, that he was a native of Porentruy, thirty-one years of age, and had been in the English service 'for a long time', serving in the Navy.

There is no one listed in the muster roll – and Najac had it in his possession – with a name even remotely resembling 'Dominique Gunay', and the man probably realized he was in an extremely dangerous position. By admitting he was French by birth, he risked being accused of being a traitor, unless he could prove that he had been unable to escape. There is little doubt that he was in the muster roll under another name, but by assuming the name Gunay he had, unwittingly, cheated himself out of his share of the prize money.

Answering further questions about the mutiny itself, Gunay said that he had been on board the *Danae* when she sailed from Plymouth on 2 March.

He was asked: 'By what means did you seize the ship?'

'Part of the crew mutinied. I joined them and we seized the arms chest and the watch [i.e. watchkeepers] to make ourselves masters of the ship.'

'How many mutineers were there?'

'One hundred and five,' Gunay said, more than doubling the actual number, which could easily be checked since both loyalists and mutineers were at Pontanezen, 'of whom five were French prisoners coming from a prize taken by the privateer *Le Malouin*, and the rest comprising foreigners making up part of the crew of the corvette.'

'What motive brought you to mutiny?'

'The bad floggings ordered by the captain were the main cause.'

'Had you all agreed to take the ship to France?'

'Yes, because there we hoped to find a refuge from the tyranny of our captain.'

His evidence had been taken down in writing, and while the three members of the tribunal signed on the left and the translator in the middle, Gunay signed his name on the right at the foot of the page.

The next witness was the Irishman who gave the tribunal the name of Ignatius Finey but which was spelled 'Fieney' in the muster roll. He said he was twenty-five years old and had been a cook in the *Danae*. He was 'sworn to relate the circumstances which accompanied and followed the mutiny in the corvette'.

After relating how the ship left Plymouth he said that: 'Having received along with his mates, all sorts of bad floggings by Captain Proby, they planned the project to overpower the ship and take her to a French port, where they hoped to find refuge and safety.

'On 14 March [sic: nautical time] at 9.30 in the evening, being five or six leagues to the north of St Mathieu, they carried out this mutiny and seized the arms chest, seizing in the enterprise the captain and other individuals who did not take part in the mutiny; that later in the morning they found themselves at the entrance to the Chenal du Four and entered it, but the calm having surprised them, they anchored in the road of Le Conquet where the corvette *La Colombe* sent them help, some men and some food.'

Having given the Tribunal his name as 'Finey', the man then signed his evidence, 'Igns Feeney'.

The third man called was William Jackson, the leader of the mutiny. He told the tribunal that he was a native of Marblehead, near Boston, 'although living usually at Liverpool', and that he was twenty-five years old. When he joined the *Danae* on 1 July 1799, as a volunteer, 'Liverpool' was entered in the 'Where born' column, and it is a coincidence that John Williams, who seems to have been Jackson's second in command and who came from the *Bordelais*, was listed in the *Danae*'s muster roll as coming from Boston.

After giving the personal details, Jackson told the tribunal that 'driven by the bad flogging by the captain' and because he wanted his freedom, he was a mutineer with his mates and made himself master of the ship when she was about five leagues to the north of St Mathieu, sailing the *Danae* to Brest after receiving men and food from the *Colombe*.

At the end of his evidence, against a cross, is written 'The mark of William Jackson'.

In the meantime, Najac had sent one of his staff to Pontanezen to interrogate Lord Proby, who was described in the report to Najac as 'a young man of about twenty years'. Proby gave a clear description of the mutiny, saying that he had about one hundred men on board at the time of the mutiny, and that the mutineers numbered about thirty-seven. He described how he was wounded while trying to climb up the hatchway, how the mutineers gained control and, to his despair, the wind allowed the mutineers to steer the ship to Le Conquet. 'Thus,' said the report, 'Captain Proby gave up his sword to an officer of the Republic and not, said he, to the mutineers.'

The report added that, according to Proby, the mutiny was principally brought about by five men from a French privateer (the *Bordelais*) who were taken on board the frigate as Americans. Among the rest of the ship's company, he added, there were 'a certain number of rascals who were attracted to French principles'.

*Ordonnateur* Najac also received the report of *Capitaine de frégate* Julien, commanding *La Colombe*. Since the French Navy did not start the new day at noon, Julien dated his report 14 March. He told how:

At midday, a ship's boat came carrying reversed English colours with the French flag above, with four English and one French men on board. They made the following report:

That they had embarked at St Malo on board the privateer *Le Malouin* which had taken a prize in which the five were put aboard [as prize crew]. They were taken by an English frigate, the *Danae*, carrying 20 guns of 32 pounds, commanded by Lord Proby.

That together with thirty-five English, they had planned a mutiny and that on the 23 Ventôse, at 9 in the evening, the rest of the crew being abed, and finding the occasion favourable, they overpowered the officer of the deck, threw him in the great cabin, barricaded all the hatchways, took possession of the arms and finally after some pistol shots and swordplay, made themselves masters of the deck, and altered course for Le Conquet. There they took two French pilots to set a course for Brest, but the calm and the end of the ebb tide prevented them doubling Pointe St Mathieu.

Because they did not have food available and not enough men

to resist for long those below, they came to ask us for help and food, not having eaten since the night before.

Consequently the captain kept the five men as hostages, sending Citizen Ollivier, *Lieutenant de vaisseau*, to verify the report and orders to take possession of the ship.

Lieutenant Ollivier arrived on board the *Danae*, confirmed the men's story and made an agreed signal back to Captain Julien in the *Colombe*. Julien sent over a boat full of armed men under *Enseigne de vaisseau* Verchin. They called on Lord Proby and his officers to surrender and 'seeing the impossibility of resisting our forces', they did.

A breeze came up, Julien added, allowing the *Colombe* to weigh and then anchor closer to the *Danae*. 'Captain Lord Proby and his first lieutenant came on board the *Colombe*,' Julien added, 'and in giving up his sword to me said: "I surrender myself to the French Navy and not to the mutineers of my ship. I would sooner perish, as would my first lieutenant, than surrender myself to them."'

Julien then sent more men to help search the prisoners, 'who were replaced by thirty men from our ship to navigate the prize, which remained under the command of Citizen Ollivier'.

The news that the *Danae* had arrived at Le Conquet and surrendered herself was, as soon as it arrived in Brest, sent to Paris by telegraph and appeared in the *Moniteur* (as described on p. 2).

The telegraph had been built by the Navy in 1794, at the outbreak of the war with Britain, and started at Chiappe, part of Brest. Messages could be passed more than three hundred miles to Paris in under one hour.

There was another telegraph line running along the coast southwards to Bayonne, on the Spanish frontier, and also uninterrupted northwards to Dunkirk. This linked every French port between Flanders in the north and the Spanish border in the south.

As soon as the news was received at the Ministry of Marine in Paris, the First Consul, Bonaparte, was informed. As Najac mentioned in his signal, Bonaparte immediately decided that he wanted to meet the five French sailors from *Le Malouin* and some of the men from the *Danae*, and Najac arranged for William Jackson, John Williams and Ignatius Fieney to travel to Paris with only four of the five Frenchmen who could be found – Jean-Marie Cochet, Jacques Arondel, Jacques le Breton and Jean Anger.

What Bonaparte had to say to them is not recorded, but the Minister of Marine, Pierre-Alexandre-Laurent Forfait, wrote to *Ordonnateur* Najac on 13 April: 'I have paid to each of these sailors, in Paris, 72 francs on account of their part in taking this prize. You would do well to take note,' he wrote, 'that this sum should be held back when the accounting is made on their return to Brest.

'At the same time I inform you that the five [sic] French sailors will be returned to their respective quarters and the Americans sent to Bordeaux, with safe conducts, and put under the authority of the Third *Arrondissement.*'

Forfait's letter, however, listed the men by name in the body of the letter, and while the Frenchmen were described as 'Of Port Malo', the others were noted as 'Irish or American'.

But that was far from the end of the affair. Five weeks later, the Minister of Marine was writing to Najac that:

Citizen Gruiloire, lieutenant of gendarmes, who was ordered to accompany as guard as far as Paris the citizens who took part in the capture of the English frigate *Danae*, has sent me an expenses account amounting to 2,421 francs, against which I have paid him in Paris the sum of 1,800 francs. I send you a copy of this account of expenses: the original stays in my office against the payment made to him. I would be obliged if you would examine it and if necessary stop payments.

The passports which Najac had issued to the mutineers were the next things to cause problems. In France at this time a Frenchman needed a passport to travel between any one town and another, a separate passport for each journey, and they were examined by the gendarmes posted at all the entrances to a town, as well as in sudden checks made on travellers by mounted gendarmes who patrolled the roads.

Since the mutineers were in fact foreigners who had never before possessed any French documents, the passports issued to them had to be specially worded and printed, and valid for any town the men might want to visit. The actual passport ended up by being a declaration by the Commissioner of the Marine certifying that the holder (whose name was filled in in handwriting) 'coming to the port of Brest in the English frigate *Danae* in which he was forced to serve, is one of a number of men forming part of the crew who contributed to the mutiny in the said frigate and brought her to France, and he has received as reward for his conduct at Brest, the sum of 72 francs.'

By the time the passports were issued, most of the men were staying in Bordeaux at various numbers in *Les Bains du Chapeau Rouge*. The paper on which the passport was printed was headed 'Bordeaux' over the word 'Marine', and '*République Française Marine*'.

Before they left Brest for Bordeaux, each man was interviewed and asked what he wanted to do. The French government had already decided that none of them should be accepted for service in the French Navy for the very good reason that men who had mutinied and carried their own ship into an enemy country could not be relied upon to stay loyal to France.

The first name on the list of men was John Williams (with the note against his name 'Pass to Paris'), listed as a gunner of American nationality. Under 'Observations' was written: 'Living at Bordeaux and sailing for three years in privateers from that place. Made prisoner from the *Bordelais* privateer. The captain of the *Danae* forced him to serve. Says he married at Bordeaux.'

Samuel Scarborough, listed as American, claimed: 'Taken from the *Bordelais* and asks to return to Bordeaux to receive his part of the prize money.' The next three men were also originally from the *Bordelais* and made the same request. The sixth man in the list, marked 'Pass to Paris', was William Jackson, the ringleader. He too claimed to be an American and said he had been taken from an American vessel called the *Betsy* at the entrance of the harbour in Guernsey. 'He asks to go to Bordeaux or other towns to serve in a merchant ship.'

The seventh man on the list said he was Irish and asked to serve in merchant ships, while the eighth, a topman who gave his name as Samuel Guillelan, claimed to be an American and asked to be sent to America. The *Danae*'s muster roll identified him as a twenty-eight-year-old Irish able seaman called James Gilliland.

Some of the names and requests told stories of simple men who had become mixed up in events far beyond their capacity to comprehend, giving false names and fortunate that the French authorities did not check them against the muster roll. One man gave his trade as blacksmith and name as William Forgeron, though he might as well have chosen 'Bellows'. He 'asks to work at his occupation'. The next name on the list was of George Taylor, yet another assumed name. He said he was a ploughman and asked 'to stay in France and work on the land'. One man claiming to be a Canadian, Charles Gaudrau in the list and down in the *Danae*'s muster roll as Charles Goodrough, and with 'France' in the 'Where born' column, had in the 'Observations' column of the French list a cryptic comment: 'Asks to return to New England. I believe him to be French.'

The majority of men asked to serve in merchant ships, but William McLuggage, 'weaver in cloth', wanted to stay in France to work as a weaver. An Irishman, Richard Galvin, said he was a ploughman and asked to work on a farm, as did David Murphy. Thomas Ferris – another adopted name – claimed to be an American and also a weaver, and wanted to stay in France and work in weaving.

The mutiny had wrought many changes in names and nationalities. Out of forty-one men interviewed by the French, twenty claimed to be Irish and twelve American. Only five said they were British. The men from Altona and Copenhagen asked to serve in merchant ships.

## CHAPTER TWELVE

# THE SALE
# OF THE DANAE

*B*y this period in the war, the exchange of prisoners between France and Britain was taking place on a regular basis, usually a man-for-man arrangement, a seaman being exchanged for a seaman, a lieutenant for a lieutenant. By chance, a cartel was due to leave Brest a few days after the *Danae* arrived, carrying other British prisoners who were to be taken to Plymouth and exchanged for Frenchmen. The French authorities decided to send to England in the cartel Thomas Hendry, the *Danae*'s surgeon, Thomas Mills, the purser, and Samuel Giles, who was the captain's clerk. There is no indication why they should have chosen these men, but of course the news of the mutiny had already reached London by way of the report in the *Moniteur*.

Proby promptly wrote a letter to their Lordships at the Admiralty for Thomas Hendry to deliver to the port admiral as soon as he arrived in Plymouth. Dated 18 March, four days after arriving at Le Conquet and three days after being imprisoned at Pontanezen, the letter told their Lordships that 'about half past nine o'clock on the 14th [nautical time] of the said month when all the officers except myself, the Marine officer and the master were in bed, the Marine officer came to my cabin to inform me there was a mutiny upon deck . . .' He went on to describe his attempt to get up the hatchway and the slash on the head which stunned him, going on to report how next day 'about 2 p.m. a large detachment of French troops came on board and as there was no longer the most distant prospect of doing my country a service by further opposition, I surrendered'.

In the meantime while the cartel went to England, Proby, his officers and the loyal members of the ship's company continued to be kept as prisoners at Pontanezen. The mutineers were also housed there until they went off to Bordeaux, and a few of them could not miss the opportunity to jeer at Proby and Niven. John McDonald, the man whom the master of a transport had begged Lord Proby to take away, was particularly unpleasant to Lieutenant Niven, who had led the party of seamen who boarded the transport and brought off McDonald.

'I saw [McDonald] repeatedly, after we were on shore,' Niven said, 'and his manner was extremely insolent. He told me that I had promised him when I took him out of the transport that I would get him his pay for her and he would be damned but he would have it. He then spoke to the Frenchmen and told them I had actually received his pay and wished them to oblige me to give him money.' He frequently came to the enclosure to insult the officers, and finally Niven told the French commissary that if he did not protect them from the insults 'we should protect ourselves'.

McDonald entered wholeheartedly into the spirit of being in Republican France and the *Danae*'s master-at-arms, William White, reported how when they were marching to Dunkirk to be sent back to England, he saw McDonald and others with 'National cockades in their hats'. The loyal seamen also heard, in gossip with the mutineers, details of the mutiny. Thomas Brown, Lord Proby's servant, told later how he had heard John Williams describing the oath they had taken on the Bible in the *Danae*'s foretop.

Thomas Olding, who had been the *Danae*'s armourer and was imprisoned with the other loyalists at Pontanezen, when asked later if he had talked to John Williams, made an intriguing reply: 'He came to the gate [at Pontanezen] with a petticoat belonging to my wife and said he was sorry for what had happened and wished me well.'

Two of the loyalists took the opportunity of being at Pontanezen to change sides. Until then, John Finley, a twenty-eight-year-old Irishman from Dublin and one of the sailmaker's crew, and George Williams, a sixteen-year-old from Bristol who was in the muster roll as a boy, 3rd class, had been with the loyalists, not having joined the mutiny. But after a few days at the prison, according to Lieutenant Niven, they 'joined the mutineers, declaring themselves to be of their party and received, in company with the other mutineers, money from the French commissary'.

The money was, of course, the 72 francs which *Ordonnateur* Najac had decided to give each of the mutineers. Asked later how he knew about the money, Lieutenant Niven related that: 'The French commissary said they received each six louis. John Marret said they were paid each three louis and that they, the mutineers, had passports given them to go to different seaports, except Jackson, who had served in the *Pompée*, Williams, one of the men taken from the *Bordelais*, and Ignatius Fieny, who had been an Irish priest and a lieutenant in the rebel army, which three were sent to Paris.'

The prisoners had been at Pontanezen for five days when a roll call was taken of everyone confined there. The heading of the roll described why it was being made: 'A List of prisoners of war at Pontanezen on 30 Ventôse year 8 [20 March 1800] and due to be transferred to the depot at Valenciennes.' The first seven names were of the master and crew of the *Mary*, captured by *La Providence* six days earlier. Each prisoner was given a number – George Marrett, master of the *Mary*, was 2972, while Lord Proby was 2980 and Lieutenant Niven 2981, followed by the chaplain, Allsop (who had not been chosen to go to England in the cartel), and then Samuel Perkins, '*domestique de capitaine*'. Altogether sixty-nine names were listed as from the *Danae* and the list ended with five men captured in the privateer *Lord Nelson*.

The Minister of Marine, Forfait, wrote to Najac:

The intention of the Consul of the Republic [i.e. Bonaparte], Citizen, is that the captors of the corvette *Danae* should most promptly reap the fruit of their courage. In consequence, you should appoint a commission of officers of the administration to examine whether or not this ship should be kept for the service of the Republic.

From the reports which have been sent to me about the qualities of the *Danae*, I have grounds for believing that the commission will not find her suitable to be bought by the Government, mainly because of the defects in her sailing ability.

In this case it will be expedient to announce, in the usual way, the sale of this ship on a certain date, to be made without delay to allow a distribution among the captors of the prize.

Should the commission be of the opinion that the Government should buy this ship, the commission is to make a survey of her hull and her tackle, rigging, sails, guns etc., and you should pass this survey to me with the report of the commission.

Should the commission decide to buy the ship, Forfait added, he would, following the orders of the First Consul, 'take such measures for the purchase of the corvette and effect payment as promptly as the situation of the Public Treasury will allow'.

The *Danae* herself was given sea trials, to check up on a report by the lieutenant who had sailed her round to Brest from Le Conquet. A note in the French archives indicates that the decision by the Navy Board in England to equip her with twenty 32-pounder carronades had indeed spoiled her performance. It must be remembered that the French still had Laporte's original report on the ship's maiden voyage to Cayenne, and he was still on leave in the Brest area.

'The ship was considered by a commission as improper for the service of the French naval war because of her lack of speed,' the final report said. The ship was therefore put up for sale and on 4 September 1800, six months after she arrived in Brest, with the mutineers on board, she was sold for 42,799 francs to Citizen J. Berubé, acting as agent for a M. Cooper, a French citizen living at Morlaix. At this time there were shipowners of Morlaix called Cooper et Cie.

A further note says that the *Danae* (which kept the name instead of reverting to her original French name) was commissioned in December for M. Cooper by a M. Riou de Kerhalet, and Cooper set about trying to charter the ship to the French government. However, there seems to be a contradiction in the reason for the sale. This is revealed by the French records, because on 22 April Minister Forfait had written to *Ordonnateur* Najac: 'The frigate *Danae* was brought into Brest by five sailors of the privateer *Le Malouin*, aided by a part of the crew of this frigate who had risen against Captain Lord Proby: the Government, informed of the courageous action of the sailors, orders the sale of this ship should be made to their profit, and that the proceeds shall be divided among them.' The order was made within a day or two of Bonaparte meeting the group of men from the *Danae*, and the decision might have been his. In a report concerning the prize, the judgment and distribution of the proceeds the Commissioner of Marine, Citizen Jean Lafosse, wrote: 'This decision without doubt will suffice to legitimize the sale.'

The problem was that the *Danae* had no French documentation: there was no certificate of registry and therefore no record of her previous existence or owners, which in turn meant that there was no way at present of recording her sale to new owners – unless the French government's order to sell the ship could form a foundation. It was a situation neither Lafosse nor Najac had encountered before. Najac realized that the men must receive the money so, Lafosse reported, the *Ordonnateur* 'proceeded with Citizen Genay, in the presence of the principal officers of the Customs and the duly authorized representative of the crew'. The crew's representative affirmed that there were thirty-five 'captors', including the five from *Le Malouin*. This was confirmed by Captain Julien of *La Colombe*. Citizen Genay then 'called for the list of the individuals who had a right to the capture in order to be able to make the distribution as soon as the proceeds of the sale should be known'.

But, Lafosse's report continued, when all this was made public, 'several foreign seamen in Bordeaux who had been part of the crew of this frigate, surprised at not finding themselves included in the list of those who had a right to a share of the prize money', went to the civil tribunal in Bordeaux to get a judicial order preventing any payments being made until their rights were secured. However, 'the Bordeaux tribunal having recognized its incompetence, referred the interested parties to the Minister of Marine in order to provide them with an appeal against a judgment which harmed their rights.'

Lafosse noted that at the disembarkation of prisoners and captors 'some of the first may have joined the second, or it may have happened at Pontanezen. The commissioner in charge of the prison at Pontanezen, instead of furnishing the Bureau of Armaments with an exact list of the captors, furnished one which carried forty-two names and became consequently the innocent instrument of the fraud by which the five English sailors were not included in the judgment.' However, he added, the passports issued to the five men 'established their rights'.

We learn from the same source that after the Bureau of Armaments had handed over permits to the English to travel to Bordeaux, the English gave power of attorney to Citizen Berubé to attend to the administration of their prize money. But the proceeds of the sale had not been handed over to the trustee three months later, by which time the five men who had found themselves not included in the distribution had put the matter in the hands of Citizen Berubé, and this had resulted in 'the legal judgments which stopped the subsequent operation'.

The whole matter was brought to a head by a letter written by Minister Forfait to Najac.

I address to you, Citizen, a petition addressed to the First Consul by Mme Moreaux, widow of Bordeaux, and three certificates of support, in favour of three foreign sailors who were part of the crew of the corvette *Danae* and who having, it seems, contributed to her surrender, claim to be included in the distribution of the proceeds of the sale of this corvette.

I invite you to give some orders for the verification of the stated facts in this petition and the documents accompanying them, and to put right this claim if it is recognized as legitimate.

You would do well to send me an account of what is done in this regard.

The documents Forfait enclosed were affidavits sworn in front of notaries in Nantes by John Brown, Richard Galvin and John Murphy.

Lafosse, in his report which would be sent to Minister Forfait, concluded that: 'The Bordeaux tribunal having recognized its incompetence, the interested parties addressed their claim to the Minister, who has sent to the Tribunal the papers and the order to restore to the claimants their rights, if well founded.' If it was allowed that the claims of the sailors not included in the distribution were just, 'it will be necessary to amend the judgment already given and to arrange a new distribution.'

However, if the Minister or the *Ordonnateur* thought that was the end of the affair, they were optimists: the matter would still be dragging on more than six months after Lord Proby and the rest of the loyalists were back in England.

## CHAPTER THIRTEEN

# INQUEST ON BOARD
# THE GLADIATOR

*L*ord Proby and his officers and men were marched to Dunkirk early in May and put on board a cartel which took them to Plymouth. Proby went up to London (a journey taking three days by postchaise) and reported to the Admiralty. In the meantime the seamen were sent to other ships and the Marines were distributed (at least one going as a guard on board a prison ship at Plymouth housing French prisoners).

Proby wrote at once to his father, the Earl of Carysfort, who was now in Berlin with his wife and daughters as the British Minister, involved in the diplomatic manoeuvring which would culminate, ten months later, in war with the Danes at the Battle of Copenhagen. The only news the Earl had of his elder son and the mutiny up to then had been letters from Earl Spencer and Lord St Vincent and what he had read in the newspapers. It was a very worrying time for him, with his elder son in a French prison at Brest and his younger son John serving in the Army in the Mediterranean.

The Admiralty lost no time in carrying out an absolutely routine matter involving the loss of a ship: ordering the court martial of Lord Proby, his officers and the ship's company for the loss of the *Danae*.

There was a tradition concerning courts martial. Depending on which was chosen for the trial, the second-in-command at that port was given the task of being president of the court. Their Lordships decided that the trial should be held at Portsmouth, so the order was sent to Sir William Parker, 'Vice Admiral of the White and second in command of His Majesty's ships and vessels in Portsmouth and Spithead'. A minimum of five post captains had to form the court, and one of the advantages of choosing a large port like Portsmouth was that members of the court could be chosen from various ships without bringing the port to a stop.

Mr Nicholas Greetham, Admiral Parker's secretary, was appointed 'judge advocate for the time being', in effect the clerk of the court, while the members of the court were Rear Admiral John Holloway and Captains Sir Henry Trollope, Edward Thornborough, George Murray (who was within ten months to distinguish himself with Nelson at the Battle of Copenhagen), Henry D'Esterre Darby (an Irishman and one of Nelson's favourites), Francis Pickmore, Charles Tyler (to fight at Trafalgar commanding the *Tonnant*), Sir Thomas Williams, Joseph Yorke (grandson of the infamous Earl of Hardwicke, who engineered the judicial murder of Admiral the Hon. John Byng, also at Portsmouth), Thomas Wolley, Thomas Graves and Stephen Church.

There was a considerable ritual on the morning the trial began. First the ship on board which the trial was to be held – in this case the *Gladiator* – fired a gun and the 'court martial flag' (the Union Flag) was hoisted at the mizen topmast peak. Boats then brought over the members of the court, all in frock coats with swords, and all carrying their commissions. These were needed to establish the seniority of the captains, so that the most junior would be the first to be asked his verdict while the most senior would sit on the right of the president.

By the time the court assembled on board the *Gladiator* on 17 June 1800, the judge advocate had asked all the accused whom they wanted to call as witnesses in their defence and written them details of the charge they faced.

The great cabin of the *Gladiator* was an impressive sight when the court finally convened, and the presence of two admirals and eleven post captains showed the importance attached to the trial. Mutiny alarmed the Admiralty as much as fire at sea did a sailor, and the Spithead and Nore mutinies of the Fleet, and the horror of the *Hermione* mutiny in the West Indies, had happened less than three years earlier.

The thirteen officers sat themselves round a large table set athwart the after end of the *Gladiator*'s day cabin, Admiral Sir William Parker sitting at one end with Rear Admiral Holloway on his right, and the captains seated to left and right in order of seniority. Greetham, the judge advocate, sat at the other end of the table, with paper, quill and penknife and ink ready: he would have to write down everything said during the trial. Where possible, questions and statements were written out beforehand, so that they could be given to Greetham, who then numbered them and inserted the numbers in his minutes, so that he could write them later in the fair copy.

With the court seated round the table, the accused men were allowed in – Lord Proby and forty-six officers, warrant officers, petty officers, seamen and Marines. One man was reported as ill, and William Hogg, an eleven-year-old boy 3rd class from Chatham, was said to be in the hospital.

The trial started with the order for the court martial being read out by Greetham: 'Pursuant to an order from the Right Honourable Lords Commissioners of the Admiralty dated 13th June instant and directed to the President, setting forth that the Right Honourable [sic] Captain Lord Proby, commander of his Majesty's late ship *Danae* had acquainted their Lordships by his letter directed to their secretary dated the 18th of March last . . .'

The order then quoted Proby's letter, ending up with the account of his surrender. The judge advocate administered the oath to the members of the court, and then the president administered the oath to Greetham. Proby's letter was again read, this time in full, and then Lord Proby was called as the first witness and Greetham administered the oath.

The first question from the court was: 'Have you any complaint to make against any of the officers or seamen of the *Danae* who are present concerning her loss?'

It was a sore point with Proby that the men on watch when the mutiny started had not leapt to the master's help to secure the deck. 'There are six men,' he told the court, 'who had the watch on deck at the time the mutiny happened and who did not, as I am informed, make any attempt to assist the officers of the watch,* which if they had done I am of opinion they could have kept the hatchway opened until I got on deck, with the other officers who

---

* They were Hall (bosun's mate of the watch), Jones (purser's steward), Harris (topman), Jeffereys (carpenter's mate), Holmes (topman), and William Coburn (Marine sentry at the scuttlebutt). Jeffereys was in fact below in his hammock after the flogging.

were below. They [later] came below and asserted themselves to be loyal, five of them are present . . .'

The court then asked the officers: 'Is there anything that has come to your knowledge censurable or deficient in the conduct of Lord Proby in his endeavours to prevent the mutiny or recover the ship?'

'None,' answered the officers.

Greetham then recorded: 'John Hall, Jones, Harris, Jeffereys and Holmes were then ordered into custody.'

The rest of the seamen were then asked if they had any allegations against Lord Proby or the officers, and they all answered: 'None, they did everything they could.'

The five prisoners were asked the same question and replied: 'None in the least.'

With the preliminaries now completed, the court asked Proby if he had a written narrative. He had and he handed it to Greetham, who then read it out.

Proby started with an apology: 'If some parts of my letter to the Admiralty are erroneous, I hope the court will excuse the apparent neglect when they consider that at the time it was written I was separated from my officers and had no opportunity of learning more particulars [other] than those which came immediately under my own eye.'

He then listed where the various officers and warrant officers were at the time of the mutiny, and went on to describe the two reasons why he kept the arms chest on deck – first, that the ship often anchored off an enemy coast at night, and second, because of the risk of mutiny and crowded conditions of the ship 'it was madness to place the arms in the very berths of the mutineers'. He said he knew it could be objected that the gunroom or cabin would have been a better place, but it was necessary to remember that with 'a cabin four feet and a half in height it would be difficult, if not impossible, to store arms of any sort so as to leave room to sit at the table. I would not have troubled the Court with this explanation,' said Proby's narrative, 'if it did not appear necessary to clear myself of blame, but I will now proceed to state the occurrences which came under my observation, and the motives guiding my conduct.'

Proby told how, warned by the Marine officer, he ran to the

hatchway and was wounded, and how very soon 'it appeared that the booms were cut down on the fore and main hatchways and the after one was secured with shot and capstan bars'. Again Proby found it necessary to put in an apology: 'It may appear at first view that I was rash and imprudent in attempting to get up the hatchway without arms and before the officers could come to my assistance, but that will no longer be the case when the court is informed that in consequence of an application by the surgeon, the fore and main hatchways were laid over every night, and I hoped not only to procure a sword in the confusion but by my presence to encourage those few who might still possess some spark of honour to assist me in defending the hatchway till the officers could collect and secure the ringleaders.'

He recalled his thoughts about chocking the rudder, knocking out the scuttles and keeping a lookout, and finally having to surrender to the French troops who came on board at Le Conquet. He then described some of the seamen he had on board the *Danae* at the time, telling the court: 'Between two and three months before the mutiny happened, the *Révolutionnaire* brought a French privateer [the *Bordelais*] into Plymouth which had on board six men who called themselves Americans; they declared they were forced to serve the French, and as there was nothing to prove they were not English I took them to fill the *Danae*'s complement which was at that time very short.'

He described the measures adopted 'to prevent any ill consequences arising from their bad dispositions' and how 'all the officers had orders to watch these men narrowly'. But, he said, they behaved extremely well and eventually – with nearly thirty of the best of his men away in prizes – he had to go to sea.

After Proby's narrative was read, the *Danae*'s former master was called, and John Huntingdon was asked to confirm Lord Proby's narrative, which he did.

He was then questioned, and his answers were vague. 'Were the five men at the bar [of the court] on the deck at the time?'

'I cannot positively say,' Huntingdon answered, 'they were in the watch and Mr Herron, the mate, reported to me that the watch were present, except for one or two who belonged to the maintop.'

'Were either [sic] of the five men missing?'

'I cannot positively say.'

'Do you know of any circumstances respecting the mutiny in which these five men assisted?'

'I do not.'

'Do you know of anything in which they could have assisted you?'

'No, I had a blow which stunned me.'

When asked to describe the mutiny, he related what he could remember of the ship's position and the weather and then said: 'While walking the starboard side of the quarterdeck I was surrounded by some men, I believe four or five, the night being very dark. They pushed me forward as far as the gangway and not knowing or perceiving the matter, I asked them what they were about, when I was surrounded by more with cutlasses.

'I called out loudly to give the alarm. They cut me over the head and struck me in different places, following me aft, and being stunned with the cuts and blows I received in the head [I] was a little while senseless. When I recovered myself [I] made the best of my way down to the cabin to inform the captain and officers what was going on . . .'

The court asked why he went down the main hatchway and not the after one. Huntingdon answered: 'Because the after hatchway ladder was unshipped and the second grating [was being] put on by some of the mutineers, I believe. The first was on before, it was dark and I could not see who they were.'

The court asked: 'Do you know how many men were on deck and actively employed in the mutiny at this time?'

'I cannot positively say, it was so dark I could not see.'

'What was the number of men at the hatch?'

'I cannot recollect.'

'Did all the watch join the mutiny, except the five men who went below?'

'I cannot positively say.'

Lord Proby then asked him if, when he first saw a disturbance on deck, he called to the men of the watch 'to assist you in defending the ship against the mutineers'?

'I called out loudly for help, to make as much noise as I could, that the officers might hear below, but no one appeared.'

Although Huntingdon was almost over the gunroom at the time he was shouting, and it was a very calm night and the ship only

just had way on, it is surprising that no one ever reported hearing
him.

'Do you think that any of the watch could be at their stations,'
Proby asked, 'and not hear your summons?'

'I believe they might have heard me all over the ship,'
Huntingdon said.

Lord Proby asked him whether, if the watch had gone to his help,
he could have prevented the gratings being put on the after hatch
for long enough to get help, but the master answered: 'I cannot
positively say. I saw a vast number of men armed upon deck.'

The members of the court were curious about the arms chest,
whence the mutineers had taken all their arms. 'Did you walk as far
aft as the arms chest was usually stowed?'

'It was on the larboard side and I was on the starboard side.'

'Was it customary for the arms to be returned to the chest after
the service was over for which they were taken out and for the
chest to be locked?'

'I believe it to be customary for the arms to be returned,'
Huntingdon said, and was lucky not to be asked why the master of
the ship was not more certain.

'During the time you were upon deck, do you not recollect
having heard a noise like the breaking open a chest or unlocking it
or taking out arms?'

'No, I do not,' Huntingdon answered.

Did he know anyone active in the mutiny? the court asked.

'I cannot say. One of the Marines, Gardner, afterwards said he
was the man who cut me, and he wished he had had three or four
more cuts at me. He was captain of the maintop, I believe.'

'Were there any Marines in the watch on deck at the time?'

'I believe there was one, who is left behind.'

'Did you see the sentinel at the water cask?'

'Yes, a little while before.'

'Had he a cutlass in his hand?'

'Yes.'

'Was his name Coburn?'

'I believe it was,' Huntingdon said.

Asked about the ship's company after the mutiny, Huntingdon
answered that Lord Proby said 'there was about forty of the crew
who wished to enter the French fleet, but they were refused and

they were sent to the same prison with us, to protect them from insu':, and afterwards let out, and received six louis each.'

The next witness was Archibald Herron, former midshipman and promoted master's mate, who was master's mate of the watch at the time of the mutiny.

Lord Proby asked him the first question. 'Did you muster the five men at the bar after the calling of the watch on the night of the mutiny in the *Danae*?'

'Yes.'

'Did the five men answer their names?'

'I cannot be positive. The boatswain's mate, Hall, answered, the carpenter's mate Jeffereys, answered, all the foretopmen answered, some of the maintopmen did not answer. Their names are Jackson and Nicholls, they were mutineers. I do not recollect that Jones and Harris answered.'

'Did you report them absent?'

'No. Harris was below in his berth, I believe.' (Herron was mistaken about Jeffereys, who had been flogged and was in his hammock.)

Asked what he was doing when the mutiny started, Herron said he was walking on the starboard side opposite the gunroom skylight, with the master walking the same side and abreast the after hatchway. Four or five men – 'Jackson was one; I do not know the others' – pushed Huntingdon forward to the gangway, 'when many others, upwards of a dozen of them, seized the master and struck him with their cutlasses, at the same time he hollering out loudly, "What, what is the matter? What does all this mean?" He sung out, "Help, help, what do all this mean?"

'I was going fast to Mr Huntingdon's assistance when I was stopped by fourteen or fifteen armed men with cutlasses in their hands and pistols in their waists, crying "Down with you, down with you, or we'll knock your damned head off, the ship is ours now and we are masters."

'Then I looked round to see if there were any on the deck but mutineers. I saw none that offered to come to my assistance, the people still threatening me with the same words and cutlasses brandishing over my head, I going to the after hatchway with reluctance, seeing there could be nothing done.'

Herron said he saw Lord Proby come running up the after

hatchway ladder but when he was within one step of the top he saw one of the mutineers – he thought it was Brown III, the black man – 'strike him with a cutlass on the head (he had no hat on) and down the captain tumbled to the foot of the ladder. They then pushed me below with their cutlasses. At that moment they dropped the grating on the after part of the hatchway, the other was on before.'

Proby then asked him, referring to the five men at the bar: 'Do you think it possible that if they were at their stations upon deck, they would not have heard the officer of the watch cry out for assistance?'

'They must have heard,' Herron said.

'If those five men and the Marine who was sentry at the water cask with the officer of the watch had joined you at the head of the hatch, how long do you suppose you could have kept the hatch open?'

The answer was not what Proby had hoped for. 'Not long. I believe there were sixteen or better men around, and seemingly very desperate.'

The court asked: 'Do you think Lord Proby could have got up?'

Herron said: 'He might have got up in the scuffle, I believe.'

Then the court asked Herron about the five men being later found below after being on watch on deck. 'Do you know what time they were discovered to be below?'

'No, they came one after another into the gunroom and gave themselves up. It was soon after I was below.'

'Did many of the watch come below?'

'Twenty-nine of the starboard watch were mutineers. The watch consisted of thirty-five exclusive of two Marines, the sentry at the scuttlebutt who came below and joined them the next day when they were taken out [by the French].'

The court asked if it would have made any difference if the five men had armed themselves.

'They had men at the arms chest abaft who refused arms to any but their own sort. I saw them aft.'

Later the court asked: 'After you mustered the watch, did the men appear to go to their respective stations?'

'They appeared to me to be as usual, some sitting on their guns, some in the galley, and others walking about.'

'Did the binnacle light give sufficient light to see the man at the wheel and the quartermaster?'

'Yes,' Herron said.

'When the master called for assistance did you observe what became of the man at the wheel and the quartermaster?'

'Yes, I saw them leave the wheel, but I did not see them afterwards. Cochrane was the quartermaster and Fleming was at the wheel.'

The court then returned to the matter of the arms chest. 'How far was the place where you were to the place where the arms was stationed?'

'About ten or twelve feet.'

'How can you account for their coming to the arms chest and procuring arms, considering your station, without your knowledge?'

Herron's answer was far from clear. 'The master singing out for assistance, I was going forward first when I was stopped by fifteen or sixteen of them armed. I do not know how they got them; they got more of them that watch.'

'Where do you suppose they got the arms?'

'One gunner's mate, Barney McGuire, and two of the gunner's crew, Brown III and Williams, who called themselves Americans, were mutineers and might have procured them for them.'

'Did you hear any person tell the quartermaster and man at the wheel to leave their stations?'

'No. There was such a murmuring noise that I could not have heard it if it had been so.'

'Did you at any time consider the quartermaster and man at the wheel as part of the mutineers?'

'I had no suspicion of them at the time but afterwards they proved that they had been concerned, for they both stayed on deck all night. After we had given ourselves up they wished to be made prisoners of war, they said they were forced upon by the people. Cochrane went immediately along with the mutineers. Fleming would not leave the ship's company, but on our coming away from France, at Dunkirk, he deserted from us.'

The court asked: 'Do you suppose that every person unconcerned with the mutiny could have escaped below?'

'Yes,' Herron said.

'Was Brown, the black man, one of the men who had been taken out of a French privateer?'

'Yes, they all six joined the mutineers. There was another Brown belonging to the gunner's crew who said he belonged to the *Hermione*.'

With the name of that ship spoken, it must have crossed the minds of the captains forming the court that at least in the *Danae* mutiny no lives had been lost: at least the mutineers had kept to their ringleaders' oath not to take lives.

Lord Proby then asked Herron to name those he thought were the ringleaders of the mutiny. 'John Brown and John Williams, two of the gunner's crew, and Jackson, the captain of the maintop, who seemed to take chief charge of the vessel. Black Brown was another. They were all, except Jackson, out of a French privateer.'

Although Herron did not say it, they were all – including Jackson later – claiming to be Americans.

The next witness called and sworn was Charles James Niven, who had been the *Danae*'s first lieutenant. Proby questioned him.

'Do you recall when so many men were sent away in prizes, my ordering you to watch [i.e. put in watches] the idlers and officers' servants?'

'I do and I put it in execution.'

Proby then asked him about the five men at the bar. 'How many of those were stationed in tops?'

'Two of them, Holmes and Harris.'

After asking Niven about the position of the after hatch, Proby reverted to the point which had become almost an obsession. 'If the five men at the bar had joined the master, the mate and the sentry at the scuttlebutt with what arms they could collect, handspikes or crows on the deck, is it your opinion they could have guarded the hatchway till the officers came to their assistance?'

Niven had never been up on deck so it was a hypothetical question and the first lieutenant said guardedly: 'From what I heard the officers say who first gained the hatchway, I think they could. It was Mr Stevens, officer of the Marines.'

The court then wanted to know: 'The five men, where did you see them first below?'

'Four of them near the gunroom door and Harris looking about the armourer's bench for cutlasses.'

'Did they tell you how they came off the deck and for what purpose they were below?'

'They said they had no hand in the mutiny and gave their names in to the officer who was taking names.'

'Did they express any wish to you or any officer to your knowledge to join with them to endeavour to recover the ship?'

'Jeffereys expressed no wish but was very active in bringing the carpenter's tools aft to chock the rudder, and Harris was looking for arms and brought some out of the midshipmen's berth (he was the midshipmen's servant).'

The court asked if any of the *Danae*'s crew had been forced to stay in France.

'None but by illness,' Niven said. 'Francis Flintiff was left sick at the hospital at Valenciennes, another boy Collis at the hospital at Fleurmell and the boy Jones.'

'Did you have any conversation with the mutineers after the mutiny?'

'While we were confined at Pontanezen, Cotes, the maintopman, came into the yard where we were confined and was excessively insolent, I cannot recollect any particular expressions except making use of the word "bugger" often. It was directed at the officers.'

Now the first of the five men at the bar was called upon to make his defence. John Hall, the bosun's mate of the watch, described how he had been going aft with a lanthorn when William Jackson met him with a cutlass and McDonald, captain of the foretop, took away the lanthorn. Hall said they told him they meant to take the ship to France and asked him to join them. Hall related how he had refused and gone to the fore hatchway and how he had got down to be asked by the sentry to get some lanthorns and candles.

James Jones, the purser's steward, told the court how he had been the lookout on the larboard gangway when he heard a noise he thought was caused by the men doing their duty. Then, in a light shining up the after hatchway, 'I saw a number of men armed with cutlasses and pistols. They drove Mr Herron, the mate, off the deck and black Brown called for Edwards, one of the carpenter's crew and a mutineer, to come and lay the after grating on.'

Jones told how he had heard William Jackson say: 'We have got the ship now in our possession and we will take her in to France.

The first man who attempts to come up the hatchway I'll blow his brains out.'

William Jeffereys told the court: 'At the time of this happening I was in my hammock asleep. The first man I spoke to was John Hall after he jumped down from the deck.' He described how he had asked a couple of times before being answered that there was a mutiny.

The topman Thomas Holmes described how he had been in the foretop when he heard a noise, and the rattling of cutlasses made him think the ship was going to quarters. He said he saw John Elliot, captain of the fo'c'sle, who told him there was a mutiny, whereupon he had jumped down the fore hatchway ladder and reported to his officer.

The fifth man, the topman Joseph Harris, who had been below ill in his hammock, was not called on to make a defence, and the *Danae's* master-at-arms, William White, was sworn.

Jeffereys asked him the first question. 'Was I in my hammock on the evening the mutiny happened on board the *Danae*?'

'He was,' White explained to the court. 'He had [been] punished the same day and said he was sore and could not get out of his hammock to do his duty.'

The court asked White the times he made his rounds of the ship and then asked: 'Did it never occur to you that there was a premeditated scheme?'

'I had never the least idea of it,' White declared.

He described how between 9 o'clock and half past he had been sitting between the fore and main hatchways, and during that time the only thing that happened was that when a man jumped below and was asked who he was, he had replied 'It's me.' 'I do not know who it was,' White said.

'Did you see any of the mutineers in France?' the court asked.

'Yes, we met four of them in our march from France. They had National cockades in their hats. McDonald and Galvin were two, I believe.'

'George Taylor and John Murphy were the other two,' Lord Proby said.

Lieutenant Niven was recalled, and Holmes asked him: 'Did you see me below and give me a knife to cut down the hammocks on one side of the deck?'

Niven told the court: 'I had Lord Proby's order to get the hammocks cut down and gave knives to several to do so, but do not recollect whether he was one or not, for I did not look at them as I gave the knives out.'

The court then told William White to name the mutineers 'and the reason for supposing them so'.

White did not hesitate. 'William Jackson, for having heard him give orders when the ship was in the possession of the mutineers; Brown, one of the quarter gunners, from having boasted after the ship was in possession of the French, that he had belonged to the *Hermione* and was saying something of the treatment of the officers; John Williams II from being one of the crew of the *Bordelais*, a French privateer taken by the *Révolutionnaire*; George Gardner from wearing the master's coat and boasting openly that he had cut the master's head; Thomas [sic: John] McDonald for giving orders while the ship was in their possession; William Cootes ... William Moreland for having hailed the French boats and called out "*Vive la République Française*"; Brown, the captain's coxswain who was exceedingly active in giving orders to the men at the wheel. Wright steered the ship.'

White's testimony ended the first day's hearing and the court adjourned until the next day, when the first witness was Lieutenant Niven, who was asked by the court: 'Do you know of any oaths being administered in the maintop and the foretop of the *Danae* to the topmen by some of the six men you got out of the *Bordelais*?'

'I had heard there was an oath taken in the tops,' Niven said, 'but I do not know by whom it was administered. I heard the officers say they had heard there was an oath administered on the day the ship was taken, at 3 o'clock in the afternoon. I heard of it after I was in France a day or two.'

Yet another Brown, this time Lord Proby's servant and a loyal man, was called into the court and sworn. He was asked by Lord Proby: 'Do you know of any oath being administered in the maintop and foretop of the *Danae* by some of the six men got out of the *Bordelais*?'

Brown testified: 'One man, by the name of Williams I believe, after we had got on shore, said that they had taken an oath on the Bible not to do any murder but only to take the ship. That was the best of my remembrance.'

He told the court that he did not hear about it from anyone else and did not know who administered the oath, nor was anyone now in England requested to join in the mutiny.

The Hon. James Rollo, the second lieutenant, was brought into court for the first time, sworn and asked to name the mutineers, giving his reasons 'for supposing them so'.

Rollo named William Jackson first, 'from knowing his voice and hearing him frequently giving orders on deck while we were below; Brown, the quarter gunner, for the same reasons; Robert [sic: John] McDonald for the same reasons; Cochrane the quartermaster for the same reasons'.

After the second lieutenant, it was the turn of the Marine officer, and Robert Stevens was sworn. Asked the same question, he named William Jackson, Brown, Williams and McDonald, having heard their voices and later seen them through the gratings. He added: 'There was another man, Gardner, when in prison who had taken my servant's hat. He showed the hat and said, "It was I took the hat from you and I was one of the principal mutineers." There was a man, captain of the mast, Jarvis I think his name, who expressed sorrow in France, saying that if he had not been asleep on deck at the time he should not have known anything about it.'

The next man called upon to list the mutineers was Thomas Davies, the *Danae*'s carpenter. He named William Jackson, Brown the quarter gunner, Alexander Robinson, one of the fo'c'slemen, 'and Brown the black man'.

Lord Proby named William Jackson, the quarter gunner Brown, his coxswain Brown, and Brown the black man, Charles Goodrough, Alexander Robertson, John McDonald and Carl Leitof. He told the court, 'I suppose that Jackson, Williams the quarter gunner, and Ignatius Fieney had a principal part in planning the mutiny as on the arrival in France, when the other mutineers received their passports, those three men were sent to Paris.'

Asked if men could have joined the loyal party in France, Proby said: 'They certainly might have done it, but I heard of no wish to that purport till they had had time to feel they were not likely to be so well treated by the French as they expected. Then there were hints thrown out by many that they were not concerned but were forced to remain on deck.

'From the time of their arrival in France, the agents of the

[French] Government, though they expressed their abhorrence of the treason, gave the mutineers some encouragement, as they acknowledged to me, in the hopes of getting possession of our whole fleet in the same way, but they absolutely refused to enter the mutineers aboard the French fleet, saying that those who would betray their own country were not likely to serve them well, and I believe from the time the mutineers were turned out of the prison with six louis and a passport to go where they pleased, they could not find a home whose inhabitants would receive them, this I suppose from knowing that they were frequently obliged to apply to the Government for shelter.'

'Did every man who stayed in France, of the mutineers, receive passports from the French Government?' the court asked.

'I believe all of them,' Lord Proby answered. 'Some of the men who did not join in the mutiny left us on the march to Valenciennes.' He named two men, one of whom left them at Dunkirk, who 'was on deck during the mutiny and I suspect has some concern in it'.

Lord Proby's evidence was the last the court heard, and the *Gladiator*'s cabin was cleared of everyone except the two admirals, eleven post captains and the judge advocate. They considered what they had heard – clearing the five men, incidentally.

The court then agreed:

That the loss of His Majesty's late ship *Danae* was caused by a mutiny of part of the crew which took place on board her about half past nine o'clock in the evening of the 14th March last, who obtained possession of the ship and navigated her to Conquet in France, and there delivered her up to French troops; that Captain Lord Proby, his officers and those of the ship's company present, and whose names are stated in the minutes, made every exertion in their power to quell the mutiny and preserve His Majesty's said ship, and did judge them to be acquitted.

The minutes of the trial concluded: 'The court was again opened, and sentence passed accordingly.'

# CHAPTER FOURTEEN

# REVOLUTIONARY RED TAPE

While the court martial of Lord Proby and his men had been held on board the *Gladiator*, the mutineers in France were getting more and more wrapped up in red tape. At first, everything had gone smoothly – Forfait had written to *Ordonnateur* Najac that Bonaparte had ordered the prize money for the *Danae* to be shared among the mutineers and the five men from *Le Malouin*. Forfait had also said that Najac should form a commission to decide whether or not the *Danae* was a suitable ship to be bought for service in the French Navy, and the commission had decided that she was 'not suitable' for government service and she had been put up for sale. All that had proceeded smoothly, and the ship had been sold to Cooper et Cie of Morlaix.

As Forfait wrote to Najac, he had heard that this money had been paid to thirty-five individuals. The money was paid out to the men named in a list supplied by the commissioner of the hospital at Pontanezen, and as soon as the names were published, several mutineers who had left Brest for Bordeaux claimed that they were entitled to a share but had not been included, so they appealed to Bonaparte.

At that point the money was tied up in red tape.

Until then, matters had proceeded quickly. A commission at Brest considering the prize had read the interrogation of Lord Proby, the report of the captain of the *Colombe*, and questioned the five Frenchmen, and concluded that:

the crew of this corvette had much to complain of because of the captain's bad treatment of them. Each day, for minor faults, he made them undergo the most rigorous punishment. The discontent was carried to the highest pitch, and was only waiting for one more episode to explode. This was not long in arriving.

Several days after the departure of the corvette from the port of Plymouth, she captured near the island of Jersey a prize made by the privateer *Le Malouin*, which had put five men on board.

Hardly were the five French prisoners on board the English corvette than many sailors of her crew consulted them on the possibility of seizing the ship and taking her into one of the French ports. The Frenchmen did not hesitate and put themselves at the head of the mutiny in spite of the danger of such an enterprise, and made efforts to feed the spirit of the discontented men.

The commission's report did not describe how prisoners of war under guard could be so active, but went on to relate how the mutiny took place. Finally, the commission warned that 'this order cannot be sufficient title for the purchaser to obtain registration of his ship. This must be based on a judgment forming the deed of ownership for whoever buys the ship.'

The mutineers had in the meantime appointed various lawyers to act for them, so that when the prize money was paid over by J. Berubé et Cie, it was split up among various lawyers acting as trustees for the *Danae* and her new owner, Cooper et Cie.

Men like John McDonald, William Moreland and the black man Brown, a total of eighteen, had appointed Citizens Potty, *Père et Fils*; Citizens Harmensen et Cie acted for another Brown, Richard Galvin and two others, while John Williams was the only client of Crevel et Chapman. There were various other proxies, and a total of 42,799 francs 73 centimes was to be distributed.

The money was to be paid in a variety of ways: there was a draft drawn on the bankers Dupont and Buguet, of Paris; ten drafts issued by Berubé and drawn by Cooper et Cie on Doyens et Cie, Paris bankers; 301 francs 23 centimes paid in coin at Brest; and Gabarus and Bechade, merchants of Brest, made a further payment.

It was at this point that the Bordeaux sailors who had been left out of the distribution went to their lawyers and, through widow Moreau, petitioned the First Consul. Soon after Minister Forfait wrote to *Ordonnateur* Najac, ordering him to look into the matter, it was also discovered that there had been a mistake: under the Act of 3 Brumaire year 4, article 17, five centimes per franc should have been withheld from the prize money towards a fund for invalid French soldiers and sailors. This was carelessness on the part of Berubé, the Minister wrote, but that was not all: apart from the five per cent for the invalids, Berubé had not paid the Treasury the one half per cent to which it was entitled. Everything had been done for the sailors and nothing for the invalids, Forfait grumbled. 'I have seen with surprise what delays have been met with in the payment of money due on this prize,' he said, and now the distribution was suspended, although Forfait said he regarded the payment as 'a sacred duty'.

He signed the letter and then added a postscript: 'I beg you not to hide the fact that the Government is very little satisfied at the slowness of the port of Brest in this affair.' He reminded Najac that the only political considerations were covered by the Acts.

Although *Ordonnateur* Najac had paid them seventy-two francs in early April, eight months later the mutineers still had not received any more money because of the delays with the prize payment. On 26 November William Jackson and Ignatius Fieney signed a power of attorney in favour of their landlord.

Before the public notary at Bordeaux appeared the undersigned William Jackson, English sailor of the English corvette *Danae* seized by the crew, living at Bordeaux, *chez* the Commissioner Poty, *père*, at Château Trompette, opposite the Baths of the Red Hat, number 135.

And Ignatius Fieney, Irish sailor, coming from the same corvette and lodged with the said Citizen Poty, *père*, who make and appoint as their general and special agent the said Commissioner Poty.

In fact both men were changing their lawyers, giving Poty the authority to settle with the commissioner dealing with the matter for their share of the prize money due 'for the sale of the corvette and its fittings, to receive all accounting of the money and verify all accounts of the sales'.

Jackson revoked the proxy previously given to Commissioner Crevel. He also asked for money due to him from 'the cruise he made in the privateer *Le Brave*, commanded by Captain Despiet'. This included pay 'for the cruise he has just made in the said privateer' and his share of the money from the prize taken 'while he was on board the said privateer'.

The proxies were 'Executed in the dwelling of the said Commissioner Poty in the presence of Commissioner Joseph Desvillère, sworn interpreter of the English language who has dictated the account of the said applicants and has read to them the present document, which they have signed before the said Commissioner Desvillère and the said notary . . .'

So at least one of the mutineers, Jackson, had gone to sea in a privateer, and we can only conclude that it was because he had long since spent his seventy-two francs. But Jackson was lucky; at the time that he and Fieney were signing the power of attorney with Commissioner Poty opposite the Baths of the Red Hat in Bordeaux another of the mutineers had already had a noose put round his neck.

## CHAPTER FIFTEEN

# THE PRICE
# OF MUTINY

'Plymouth, 26th August 1800,' Lieutenant Niven's letter began and, addressed to a Captain John Wickey, it said:

I beg leave to inform you of my having found among the French prisoners in Mill prison, John Maret [sic: Marret], a seaman belonging to His Majesty's late ship the *Danae* and who I saw in the mutiny, armed with a pistol and cutlass guarding the after hatchway, which the mutineers had secured.

I am sorry to inform you that I have not been able to discover any more of the *Danae*'s men on board the prison ships I have visited, and I shall finish my search by overhauling the Caton tomorrow, which I should not be able to do this evening in time for the post. I have also, agreeable to your order, looked at the two men on board the *Cambridge*, but I am sorry they are not any of the Danaes.

The Lords Commissioners of the Admiralty had not forgotten the *Danae* or her mutineers. Her captain, officers and loyal men had been cleared by a court martial, but their Lordships knew one important thing about the mutineers: most of them were seamen, and with few exceptions seafaring was the only life they knew. It was inevitable that in time they should serve in French ships and equally inevitable that some of them would be captured, and, although they might hide their identity for a time, sending one of the *Danae*'s officers to inspect the inmates of places like Mill Prison at Plymouth and the prison hulks moored in the Hamoaze and up the River Tamar would in time yield results.

Lord Proby's journal for November records that the *Danae* was at sea with Lord Bridport's fleet towards the end of the month, and on the morning of 26 November made the signal for setting up the rigging. In the afternoon is the cryptic entry: 'Chased and boarded Jersey privateer, impressed 15 men.' One of the fifteen was a twenty-eight-year-old Jersey man, John Marret. At first he refused to take the bounty and was put down in the muster roll as 'prest', being rated able seaman. (Two eighteen-year-olds also taken from the privateer, and both from Jersey, volunteered.)

Now, Marret, the mutineer who had gone to sea again from Brest or Bordeaux and still had not received his 1,145 francs 54 centimes from the French authorities as his share of the *Danae* prize money, had been captured, brought in to Plymouth, put in the prison, and then had gone through the ordeal of being lined up with the other prisoners in the Mill Prison and seeing that the officer walking along the line, having a good look at every prisoner's face, was his former first lieutenant . . .

Once again the majesty of a court martial was set in motion. An order from the Admiralty was sent to Sir Henry Harvey, Vice Admiral of the White and second-in-command at Plymouth, to hold a trial to try Marret.

The court assembled to try him was a distinguished one – there were three admirals in addition to Harvey: Vice Admiral Sir Andrew Mitchell, Rear Admiral Sir Charles Cotton and Rear Admiral Sir Robert Calder. Among the nine post captains were Captain John Wickey, who had sent Lieutenant Niven to the Mill Prison in the first place, George Murray, who had sat at the trial of Lord Proby (and was within weeks of being sent to the Baltic for the forthcoming Battle of Copenhagen), Sir Thomas Boulden Thompson (who had distinguished himself at the Nile and was to lose a leg at Copenhagen) and Philip Durham, who was to command the *Defiance* at Trafalgar.

Robert Liddel was appointed deputy judge advocate, and he sent Marret the charge and a request that he name witnesses he wished to call in his defence.

On 2 September, after the gun had fired and the Union Flag had been hoisted at the mizen peak on board the *Cambridge*, the trial began with the deputy judge advocate reading out Lieutenant Niven's letter addressed to Captain Wickey. Niven by now had a command of his own, the hired armed brig *Sir Thomas Pasley*, whose presence in Plymouth had led to Captain Wickey's original order.

All the witnesses were ordered to withdraw from the *Cambridge*'s great cabin and Niven was called first and sworn. He identified Marret as belonging to the *Danae* during the mutiny and was told: 'Relate to the court the most circumstantial account of the prisoner on that occasion.'

'I went soon after it was daylight on the morning of the 15th of March last to the after hatchway to endeavour to see the men up on deck,' Niven said. 'I found the after gratings secured with capstan bars and a sail over the gratings, but a part of the gratings was not covered with the sail, and I saw the prisoner through the part which was not covered. William Moreland stood upon the starboard side of the hatchway and the prisoner upon the larboard side with a pistol and a cutlass. I saw him also speaking to McDonald and John Brown III at the larboard gangway.'

Niven then described how he saw Marret when he and Lord Proby were taken down into a boat.

The court asked: 'How long had you been on board the *Danae* before the mutiny?'

'About twelve months.'

'How long had the prisoner been on board before the mutiny?'

'Three or four months. I pressed him out of a privateer and he afterwards said he would enter [i.e. volunteer and receive the bounty], and he was put on the bounty list but did not receive it owing to the ship sailing.'

The court asked several routine questions and then: 'Did you, when you first saw the prisoner armed and standing sentinel at the hatchway, admonish him and point out to him the predicament in which he stood?'

'As Lord Proby had directed Mr Allsop, the chaplain, to admonish them and it was thought he would have more influence with the people than his Lordship and myself, Mr Allsop went to the after hatchway and spoke to them. He was answered in an insolent manner by Jackson and McDonald. I therefore did not say anything.'

After more questions, the court asked: 'Was he forced to be a sentinel?'

'As far as I could judge of the man by his appearance when I saw him speaking to McDonald and Brown, he appeared to be smiling.'

The next witness was the former surgeon, Thomas Hendry, now serving in the *Ambuscade*. Hendry identified Marret and, asked to describe Marret's conduct, said that when taken on deck with the rest of the officers, 'I perceived the prisoner armed with one of the ship's cutlasses fastened round his waist. He was in conversation with others of the mutineers and appeared much rejoiced at the state of the ship . . .'

Asked if he thought Marret had been forced to act as he did, Hendry said: 'On the contrary. He seemed to have been very active from what I observed.'

Could Marret have joined the loyalists in France? the court asked.

'Yes, they were allowed by the French to stroll about the prison yard and might have put themselves under the protection of the officers, and two Marines did join the officers.'

The next witness was a Marine from the *Danae*, and the trial minutes record: 'Lawrence Dowling, private Marine in His Majesty's prison ship the *St Nicholas* sworn.'

'Was you serving on board the *Danae* at the time of the mutiny?' the court asked.

'I was, as a private Marine.'

'Do you know the prisoner?'

'Perfectly,' replied Dowling.

'Did he belong to the *Danae* at that time?'

'He did.'

'What part of the ship was you in when the mutiny began?'

'In my hammacoe, asleep.'

'Relate to the court all you know respecting the prisoner on that occasion.'

'At the time the mutiny broke out . . . the Corporal of Marines came to my hammacoe and begged me for God's sake to turn out, or words to that purport, if I had a mind to save my life. On which I turned out immediately, thinking the ship was on the rocks.

'As soon as I slipped on my jacket and trousers I ran directly to the after hatchway, thinking to go on deck. One of the men who was sentinel over the hatchway made a blow at me with a cutlass, on which I stepped back and looked up and saw the prisoner with a cutlass and pistol.

'I inquired of the sentinel who guarded the hatchway what was the matter. He replied, "You had better go about your business. You shall know presently," or words to that effect. Directly after that they laid over the gratings and the tarpaulin.'

Did Dowling think that Marret was forced to join the mutiny?

'I really believe he was not forced. He appeared to be a volunteer in the business. My reason for it is there was a Marine, William Coburn, sentinel over the scuttlebutt. They asked him if he would join and he refused. They therefore confined him a prisoner in the galley.'

'Had you ever any conversation with the prisoner?'

'Yes, frequently.'

'Can he speak English?'

'Yes, fluently.'

The court then asked: 'Do you know the man you spoke to at the hatchway?'

'Yes, it was William Moreland, the gunroom cook.'

'Was it him who said you should know presently?'

'Yes, and he made the blow at me with a cutlass and told me I should know presently, or words to that effect.'

With that, the prosecution had finished its case and Marret was called for his defence. He, the minutes recorded, 'had nothing to offer but a general denial of the charge and had not any evidence to produce on his behalf'.

The minutes concluded:

The court having carefully and deliberately weighed and considered the evidence produced and what the prisoner had alleged in his defence, was of opinion that the charge had been fully proved and did in consequence therefore adjudge the prisoner John Marret to be hanged by the neck until he is dead at the yardarm of such one of His Majesty's ships and at such time as the Lords Commissioners of the Admiralty shall direct.

Marret, now a condemned man, was taken back to the 40-gun frigate *Pique*, in which he was kept prisoner while the trial was on, being brought daily to the *Cambridge*.

A few days later the *Pique*'s commanding officer, Captain F. S. Young, received orders to arrange for Marret to be hanged on board his ship. The orders were long, describing the court martial on board the *Cambridge* and its verdict and sentence. They concluded: 'You are therefore hereby required and directed to see the said sentence carried into execution accordingly on Tuesday the ninth day of the month, at eleven o'clock in the forenoon, by causing the said John Marret to be hanged by the neck until he is dead, at the foreyardarm of His Majesty's ship the *Pique*, for which this shall be your warrant.'

A hanging on board one of the King's ships was a matter which was made to concern every person in the port. To begin with, a letter from the commander-in-chief was read to every ship's company. This detailed the man's crime and the sentence. Then, at ten o'clock, a gun was fired from the *Cambridge* and a yellow flag was hoisted – the signal that an execution was due to take place, and that armed and manned boats from every ship were to attend the execution.

To indicate which ship, the *Pique* also fired a gun and hoisted a yellow flag. Soon after that Marret was brought up to the fo'c'sle with the *Pique*'s chaplain, and while the chaplain ministered to him, Marret had a good view of the noose awaiting him. A block had been slung from the starboard side of the *Pique*'s foreyardarm and a long rope rove through it. The end on the forward side of the yard had a noose made up on it; the after end led aft and for the time being lay along the deck. The gun below where the noose hung was loaded and run out, the grinding of the trucks turning being, it would seem, part of the punishment.

In the meantime the boats from the other ships in Plymouth had rowed over to the *Pique* and were now gathered like so many ducklings round their mother, the lieutenants commanding them ordering the men to row or back water occasionally to keep position against wind and tide.

By 11 o'clock, Marret was standing with a black hood over his head and the noose round his neck. At the other end of the rope a couple of dozen of the *Pique*'s men now held on, ready for the order to run aft with the rope, jerking the noose end in the air.

At 11 o'clock precisely Captain Young made a signal to the gunner after reading out the charge and sentence, and the gun immediately below Marret fired, spurting up a cloud of smoke, and the seamen ran aft. Marret's body was jerked upwards to the yardarm, where it was left to hang for half an hour, a grim warning to all the watching seamen. So, a little more than six months after the mutiny, John Marret paid the price for his part in it.

At the time that Marret was hanged on board the *Pique*, those mutineers who could be found in Brest or Bordeaux were having their passports corrected. The details entered in handwriting on the printed form were as supplied by the holder of the passport. An example of the contradictions is illustrated by the passport held by Thomas Jarvis, the seaman who had complained to the Marine lieutenant that had he not been asleep on deck he would have known nothing of the mutiny.

The details about Thomas Jarvis in the *Danae*'s muster rolls – both the last one sent to the Navy Board and the latest one, then in the hands of the French – were that he joined the ship on the 28 October 1798 (and was thus one of the longest-serving members of the ship's company), that he had been born in Bristol, and that at the time that he entered the ship he was fifty-four years old, one of the oldest men on board. However, his passport (with its printed heading that it had been issued by 'the Commissioner of Marine, Clerk of the Bureau of Manning, and the Clerk of the Bureau of Registration of the port and department of Bordeaux') contradicted the muster rolls: Jarvis had now decided to become an American.

The actual passport was a printed form with spaces for the person's details to be written in. The issuing authorities, therefore, 'certify that the Citizen *Thomas Jarvis, American, weaver*, coming from the port of Brest in the English frigate the *Danae* in which he was forced to serve, is one of a number of men making up part of the crew who contributed to the uprising in the said frigate and brought her to France and who has received for his conduct and reward at Brest, the sum of seventy-two francs. Bordeaux, 17 Vendémiaire year 9.'

The problems concerning distribution of the prize money continued, with a second report being sent to Minister Forfait by the Commissioner of Marine, this one also drawn up on *Ordonnateur* Najac's behalf by Citizen Jean Lafosse. The report, intended to placate the Minister, was described as concerning the prize, the judgment and distribution of the proceeds of the sale.

'The frigate *Danae* was brought into Brest by five sailors of the privateer *Le Malouin*, aided by part of the crew of this frigate who had risen against Lord Proby,' the report began.

'The Government, informed of the courageous action of the sailors, ordered that the ship should be sold and that the amount of the proceeds should be divided among them. (Minister's letter of 22 April.)

'This decision, without doubt, should be sufficient to legitimize the sale,' the report declared. *Ordonnateur* Najac had proceeded to arrange for the sale, consulting with the principal officers of the Customs and the duly authorized representatives of the crew. It was confirmed by the captain of *La Colombe* that the number of mutineers was thirty-five, including the five Frenchmen from *Le Malouin*.

Citizen Genay, working for the *Ordonnateur*, 'called for the list of the individuals who had a right to the proceeds in order to be able to make a distribution as soon as the amount of the sale should be known'. The rights of each one of the men, the report said, would be based on his name being written on the list. This list was supplied to Najac's tribunal, and the whole transaction now being assured, permission was given for the men to go to Bordeaux if they wished.

But, the report said, when the distribution was put into operation and made public, 'several foreign sailors, reunited in Bordeaux and who had been part of the crew of this frigate, were surprised at not finding themselves included in the list of those who had a right to a share of the prize.' So, later, the Minister by his letter invited the tribunal 'to revise its judgment concerning the distribution of the prize money if the claimants' rights had any foundation. The mix-up,' the report added:

could have happened while disembarking prisoners and captors, when some of the first may have joined the second, or it could have happened at the hospital, where both groups were lodged.

The commissioner of the hospital [at Pontanezen], instead of furnishing the Bureau of Armaments with an exact list of the captors, furnished one which consequently became the innocent instrument of the fraud by which the five English sailors were not included in the judgment. Their claims, however, were legitimized by the entries on the passports that were given them.

The report explained that the five men had travelled to Bordeaux originally because they had been given permission and had also given a power of attorney to a local notary before leaving Brest. When the ship was sold, the five men received nothing because their names were not on the tribunal's list, and so they took action.

The report concluded: 'This is the analysis of the affair which is submitted to you, and the conclusion that proceeds from it is that, if you allow the claims of the sailors not included in the distribution, it will be necessary to amend the judgment already given because the payments will change owing to the number of shares.'

No sooner was this report completed than it was found that the sailors in Bordeaux who had appealed to Paris through the good offices of the widow Moreau were not the only ones left out of the prize distribution: soon they totalled eleven, and yet another report was submitted to Najac – by now it was the middle of 1801.

The problem raised by the report was quite simple: the money from the sale of the *Danae* had been distributed among the names on the first list, but with another eleven men to be paid, a further 12,611 francs 94 centimes were needed, because each man was entitled to 1,146 francs 54 centimes. This included the widow Moreau's three men, who were entitled to a total of 3,439 francs 62 centimes. The report had no useful suggestions to make, apart from advising the tribunal to look again at its decision of 18 May 1800 and observing that only the men named in the first distribution had received their money, and this distribution had used up all the money there was. The government, the report added, 'desired to recompense all the sailors who took part in the mutiny on board this frigate'.

Finally, on 16 October 1801, nineteen months after the mutiny, the prize tribunal met once again, this time with *Ordonnateur* Najac as president, sitting with four officials from the Brest dockyard as assessors.

First they examined the claim of the sailors not included in the list of those sharing the first distribution on 18 May the previous year and 'whose claims are established in the letter written to the First Consul by the widow Moreau', as well as certificates given by the under-commissioner of Marine at Brest. The tribunal acknowledged that the omissions in the first distribution did not arise through any false declarations by the sailors who, when they were interrogated, gave the number of mutineers as thirty, not including five Frenchmen.

'The tribunal, wishing to repair an error involuntarily made, decided that the number of participants in the capture of the corvette *Danae* will be forty-six, including the five Frenchmen.' Having decided that, the tribunal then ordered the original list of names to be revoked.

The tribunal then named the eleven men who were to be paid the same as the rest, the money coming from the budget of Najac. Among the men were James Cochrane, who had been quartermaster at the time of the mutiny, Barney McGuire, one of the gunner's crew and suspected of opening the arms chest, and several men who had kept their surnames but changed their first names. There were also Richard Nicholls, the twenty-seven-year-old ordinary seaman from Tonnerick, in Cornwall, Charles Goodrough (now claiming to be a Canadian and spelling his surname Gaudrau), and a Portuguese down in the muster roll as James Manuel, from Madeira, who had now become Manuel Joseph, while the rest had not been named in the mutiny or had changed their names.

So finally each man was paid 1,146 francs 54 centimes for his part in the mutiny.

In the meantime, the situation was slowly changing at sea. In April of this year Nelson had fought and won the Battle of Copenhagen, closing the blockade of French ports a little tighter by restricting the supplies of timber and rope from the Baltic.

And while the eleven men had struggled to get their share of the prize money, John Marret had been hanged and two more of their fellow mutineers were back in England, the noose dangling over their heads.

As soon as the court martial had cleared him and his crew, Lord Proby wrote to the Admiralty. It was quite common for an officer after he had been cleared of a serious charge by a court martial to publish the minutes of the court martial evidence as a small pamphlet. Proby's defence makes it clear that he considered himself to be misunderstood; although the court martial had cleared him, he appears to feel that his motives in doing what he did were not fully understood. As newspapers did not report such trials at any length, pamphlets were the accepted (and only) way of publicizing such an event.

So, staying in London at the Carysfort house in Hanover Square, he wrote to Evan Nepean on 21 June: 'I beg you will inform my Lords Commissioners of the Admiralty that I wish to publish the proceedings of the late court martial upon the officers and crew of the *Danae*, and request, if they have no objection to the publication, that they will allow me a copy of the above mentioned proceedings.'

Proby then left London to stay a few weeks at the family home at Elton Hall. He had been there some time when, receiving no reply from the Admiralty, he realized why, and wrote at once to William Marsden, the second secretary:

I have been so negligent as to leave Town without putting my address in the Admiralty book. I must therefore trouble you not to let me lose any chance of employment on that account. I am only staying here a few days and then set off for Ireland [where his father had another house].

If you will have the goodness to desire any office letter for me to be directed to Charles Osborne Esqre, Mountjoy Square, Dublin, I shall be very much obliged to you. I applied for a copy of my court martial, that I might have it printed but I am afraid there has been some mistake for I have no answer whether it will be granted or not.

There is a note written across the corner of the letter: '2 Aug. Note Lord Proby's address. Acquaint him that their Lordships having considered his request of 21st June do not think proper to allow of a copy of the minutes being given for the purpose of publication.'

Lord Proby's father in Berlin, although pleased to hear that his eldest son had been cleared by the court martial, was soon getting letters about Proby's behaviour. The Earl was due for leave some months later, and it was not until 30 July 1801 that he was able to write to Lord Grenville, the Foreign Secretary and his brother-in-law, about it. The Battle of Copenhagen had been fought and won in April, and there was less need for Carysfort's reports of what was going on in government circles in Berlin.

Carysfort said he would take his leave of absence and return about the beginning of October, 'that is, when the heats are past, the roads in good order, and we have a better chance of a steady wind for the passage.

'It would on some accounts be desirable to defer our removal until the Spring. But I have some business too urgent to be neglected, and am very uneasy of Proby's situation, who may, I fear, be still some time without a ship, and is too inexperienced not to get into scrapes if he remains without control on shore.'

The Earl had good reason to worry because Proby had at this time been sixteen months 'on the beach' without a ship.

Thomas Grenville (whose sister was married to Lord Carysfort) wrote to his brother Lord Grenville on 10 August that he had received a letter from the Earl of Carysfort in which he said he was coming home,

> partly from an anxiety which he feels about Lord Proby, who not finding a ship has found himself in love and in danger of matrimony; and partly because of the ardour of Lord Proby's matrimonial pursuits, he seems to have done less of his father's business than of his own.
>
> This is an unlucky event; and though, by Lord Carysfort's manner of speaking of it, I take for granted there is nothing decidedly objectionable about the intended lady, yet I agree with him in most heartily wishing that Lord St Vincent may terminate this embarrassment by giving him a tight frigate, instead of leaving him to provide himself with a pretty wife.

Lord Carysfort was having a worrying year. In the previous August, in 1800, just after Proby was released, Lord Carysfort had written to Mr Coutts, the banker in London:

> I have received from Lord Minto the unpleasant news that my second son, John, has been made a prisoner by the French.
>
> He was going with despatches from Melas's army to Lord Keith from Venice to Ancona in a small vessel procured at the former place. They were overtaken by a storm and whether from

that cause or from treachery is uncertain, the sailors put into Cascanatico, where he was seized and delivered up to the French.

I have sent a letter to him in France and told him he may draw upon you and that you would have the goodness to pay his draughts and charge them to me, and perhaps if you have the means of recommending him to any person in Paris it may be of use to him and I am sure you will excuse therefore my desiring you to take that trouble.

However, Lord Proby in the peace over Europe was neither wrecked on the shores of matrimony nor given another ship, although there is no hint of the identity of the young lady. He had previously written to his sister Charlotte in Berlin referring to their old Spanish governess. 'My dear Charlotte,' he wrote,

I will not plead guilty to the charge of neglect because I have verily believed you to be a great rogue, and that I wrote the last letter. I am delighted to hear that there are flower gardens in Berlin, for I had fancied such a stupid place as to have nothing but a single park, and that very miserable.

I opened Lizzy's [his stepmother's] letter to Gertrude and I find, tho' you have escaped contagion, she has all the fine airs of a Germaness . . . I am likely to have a ship immediately and with all the merry people there are about me, I should be wondrous happy, but that I hear the Spaniard is dead and I am in a violent passion (you may see it by my writing) with you for not sending her body to be buried in her country. I am very uneasy upon the object because I fear you will be haunted, because the ghost cannot be quiet among a parcel of Germans smoking and drinking and eating stewed prunes. Do pray dig the body up and send over in a bottle of brandy.

Amidst all this agitation I have found time to order my Father two coats, the pattern of which I enclose. The dark is to take white and the light one yellow buttons, and the whole to be finished in the newest taste.

Proby was wrong about his ship: he had to wait several more months for one, and in the meantime his father was trying to use his influence. Lord St Vincent had written to Lord Carysfort from the Admiralty on 14 April, 1801; 'I have had Lord Proby in my contemplation ever since I came to this Board, but there are so many officers of great merit senior to his Lordship who have been much longer out of employment, I cannot bring him forward at present without the most flagrant injustice to them.'

With the brief peace between France and Britain at the signing of the Treaty of Amiens, the world was at rest, but few knowledge-able people thought the peace would last long. However, Lord St Vincent was one of those who thought it would be lengthy: long enough for him to carry out some very sweeping and long overdue reforms in the Navy dockyards – reforms weeding out corruption which could not be undertaken in wartime. St Vincent was wrong; but for the eighteen months that the peace lasted, many post captains found themselves on half-pay while their ships were paid off.

Lord Carysfort was still very concerned that Proby would be safer at sea, and wrote again to the First Lord asking for a ship for him. Lord St Vincent answered: 'I am honoured by your Lordship's letter of 30 July and I have great pleasure in repeating to your Lordship that it is my intention to give employment to Lord Proby as soon as I can, consistently with what is due to the meritorious officers of the same rank, who have been longer on half pay.'

Earlier Proby himself had been upset by a rumour which led him to write to Lord St Vincent in the previous April, and the First Lord replied on 22 April: 'No such report as that you allude to in your letter of the 18th has reached me, and if it had would have been totally disbelieved; for I have always considered your Lordship as most sincerely attached to the profession, and I shall have great pleasure in placing you in a situation to do equal honour to your country and your family . . .'

Proby wrote again six months later, and St Vincent answered on 20 October 1801: 'Your Lordship may be assured of my disposi-tion to serve you, and that I should have given you an early appointment had the war continued. At present it is totally impossible for me to enter into any engagement with respect to the peace arrangement.'

Proby's younger sister had returned to England with the family when he wrote on 29 June 1802, and although he was writing in a light vein it seems he was still unwilling to be criticized:

> I am very much obliged to you indeed for your two letters, but I will not acknowledge myself to blame because they both came together this morning and the first is written so like John's hand that I can hardly persuade myself he has not been forging for you . . .
>
> I had a most lucky payment of prize money yesterday which I had given up as completely lost. It amounts to four guineas, and as yours and Charlotte's purses are of course a little drained by the purchase of a new watch for Fanny, I must have you share the plunder of the French vagabonds with me. You must get Abraham to take the enclosed note to Coutts the Banker and he will change it for two guineas . . .

## CHAPTER SIXTEEN

# THE TRIAL OF
# JOHN McDONALD

The first of the two *Danae* mutineers to be caught after John Marret was hanged was one of the ringleaders, John McDonald. He was court-martialled on board the *Irresistible* at Black Stakes, in the Thames, on 10 June 1801, at a time when several of the victorious ships from the Battle of Copenhagen were just arriving back in the Thames and Medway. The president of the court was Rear Admiral Bartholomew Rowley, second-in-command of the ships and vessels in 'the Medway and at the Buoy of the Nore'.

Six post captains had been chosen to form the court in addition to the president, and one of them had just returned to the Thames from Copenhagen having added to his unpopularity (and startled Lord Nelson by asking for a letter saying he had performed well in the battle). But no serving captain in the Royal Navy knew more about the effect of a mutiny; he was Captain William Bligh, who had commanded the *Bounty* until Fletcher Christian's mutiny led to Bligh making a voyage of 3,900 miles in an open boat across the Pacific, a feat which showed he was a fine seaman and navigator, if nothing else. (By coincidence another member of the court was Captain John Bligh, no relation.)

When the court opened the Admiralty order for trying 'John McDonald, alias Samuel Higgins', was read, followed by Lord Proby's letter written from Pontanezen and another from Lieutenant Niven, describing how fifteen months after the mutiny he had found McDonald walking the streets while serving in the American schooner *Bilboa* of Pennsylvania, now in the London docks. Although McDonald described at length in his defence how it happened, it seems Lieutenant Niven was walking along a street in

Wapping when he saw McDonald and promptly seized him. He was handed over to the watch and Niven wrote to Evan Nepean at the Admiralty from his lodgings in Surrey Street, the letter dated 6 pm on 4 June 1801.

The trial took the usual course. The first witness was Lord Proby, on half-pay and spending his time at his father's town house, at Elton Hall in Huntingdonshire, and at the family house in Ireland.

After identifying McDonald, Proby was asked by the court what he knew of McDonald during the mutiny.

'I was wounded and could not go about the decks as was necessary to have any chance of distinguishing the prisoner more than once or twice, when he appeared to be active and consulting with the other ringleaders. Several of the officers reported their seeing him likewise. At the time I left the *Danae* I saw him on the deck, armed, as the other mutineers were.'

'When the prisoner was armed and consulting with the ring-leaders of the mutiny,' the court asked, 'did he appear to be trying to quell the mutiny or to excite them to go on?'

'I did not overhear the conversation, but from language I heard afterwards, he was not likely to persuade them to do anything but mutiny.'

Proby said later: 'The officer of the watch reported him as one of the first that appeared armed and active in the mutiny.'

The court asked: 'When the ship's company of the *Danae* were landed, did they all go on shore together, mutineers and others?'

'Those who were with me, together with the officers, were landed at Conquet. The mutineers were landed at Brest.'

'Was it by their own desire or yours that they were separated?'

'It was the desire of the French, I believe.'

Later the court asked what was to be a critical question: 'By what name did the prisoner go on board the *Danae*?'

'McDonald, I do not recall the Christian name.'

'How long was it after the mutiny began before you saw the prisoner?'

'It might have been six or seven hours.'

'How long was it after the mutiny before you left the *Danae*?'

'About three or four o'clock the next evening.'

'Had the prisoner any arms in his hands when you first saw him after the mutiny?'

'He was armed, certainly – as near as I can recollect with a brace of pistols in his belt.'

The court asked: 'Did you hear the prisoner make use of any improper language, or did he use improper actions?'

'He used both improper language and actions at the time of my leaving the *Danae*, but I heard very little speaking of any sort during the mutiny. I do not recollect the prisoner's exact words, but I remember observing them at the time to the officers who were with me, and their making the same observations to me.'

'Were the gratings open or shut at the time of the mutiny?'

'The fore and the main gratings were partly on in consequence of an application from the surgeon. The two gratings were off the after hatchway at the first breaking out of the mutiny; but they were put on as stated in my letter, before I recovered from the stun I received in attempting to get up the hatchway.'

Later the court asked how long McDonald had served in the *Danae*.

'Not long. I cannot exactly recollect the time – he was pressed from a transport off Jersey, in consequence of the master begging I would take him out of his ship.'

'Where was you when you saw the prisoner walking about and at liberty in France?'

'I saw him through the doors of the little yard I was allowed to walk about in, being myself confined.'

'Was the prisoner at liberty to quit the place where you saw him?'

'I believe after the first day of the mutineers landing in France they had leave to go where they pleased.'

The court now turned to McDonald and asked him if he had any questions to ask Lord Proby and he, the minutes record, 'declared he did not know Lord Proby'.

Lieutenant Niven was the next prosecution witness and after identifying McDonald he was asked: 'By what name did he go on board the *Danae* at the time of the mutiny in that ship?'

'His surname was McDonald and to the best of my memory his Christian name was John.'

Niven was shown the letter of 4 June 1801 to the Admiralty and he acknowledged it was his. He was then asked about McDonald's conduct during the mutiny.

'During the night in which part of the *Danae*'s ship's company mutinied on 14 March, 1800, I heard the prisoner repeatedly call out to keep a good lookout there, which was answered by the sentinel over the after hatchway and by the other people upon deck.

'As soon as it was daylight I perceived the prisoner sitting on the larboard hammock nettings armed with a pistol and cutlass and giving orders.

'I saw the people on the after part of the quarterdeck go forward and hoist the foretopsail in consequence of the prisoner's orders, who had been previously spoken to by one of the French prisoners then upon deck.

'I afterwards saw the prisoner active in giving a rope to the French boats. On being suffered to come upon deck and put in the boat with Lord Proby, I heard the prisoner then pointing to Lord Proby make use of the words *"Noblie de Diable – noblie de merdo"* and, addressing himself to the Frenchmen, said Lord Proby gave six dozen for the royal bowlines and that it was him that cut them.'

'Where were you when you saw the prisoner active in the mutiny?' the court asked.

'Standing under the after gratings, looking through a crevice not covered by the mizen staysail, which had been thrown over the hatchway grating.'

Asked if he made any attempt to get on deck when the mutiny began, Niven said he had been in bed. 'On being called I got a dirk and ran in my shirt to the after hatchway. While going to the after hatchway I met Lord Proby returning to his cabin. I found the after hatchway secured down, and several cutlasses through the holes of the grating. The officer of Marines and, I think, the carpenter, reported the fore and main hatchways to be also secured. I then went to Lord Proby's cabin and found him bleeding from some cuts he had received to his head, and the master in the same situation.

'I then received Lord Proby's orders to cut down the hammocks and to take the names of the men below. His Lordship also desired me to order the officer of Marines to collect his party and arm them with such arms as we could find. I complied with these orders.

'Lord Proby then proposed chocking the rudder and firing up the hatchways should we discover any number of mutineers together, but upon looking at the chart and getting a compass into the cabin, we supposed ourselves in the Passage [sic] de Four and Lord Proby said it was better to stand fast chocking the rudder until we were round St Mathieu's as we would then stand a chance of being picked up by our own cruisers off the Black Rocks.

'From our situation we all agreed with his Lordship that it was better to do so, and Lord Proby desired me to knock out the bow scuttles on the larboard side and endeavour to make out what part of the Passage de Four we were near, which I did and reported to his Lordship somewhere about Conquet, and that there was little wind. On my return to the cabin, I saw the jolly boat lowered from the stern, and heard afterwards several boats approaching the ship.'

When the French boats came on board the *Danae*, the court asked, did the officers and the loyal men go on shore with the mutineers?

'The officers of the *Danae* and the men attached to them were taken as prisoners to the *Colombe*, French brig of war. The mutineers remained in the *Danae*, some taking in the sails, the others towing the French boats with us in them.'

Asked if there was anything to prevent McDonald joining the officers had he wanted to, Niven said: 'Most certainly not. A Marine named Coburn, who was upon deck during the whole of the mutiny, joined the Captain and officers at the time we were going out of the ship as prisoners, declaring that the mutineers would not suffer him to quit the deck before, and that at the commencement of the mutiny he was afraid to quit his post as sentinel over the scuttlebutt.

'Several days afterwards, while confined at Pontanezen, Finley, the sailmaker, and the boy Williams, joined the mutineers, declaring themselves to be of their party, and received in company with the other mutineers money from the French commissary.'

'Do you speak of the mutineers receiving money from your own knowledge or from what you have heard?'

'I speak from the information of the French commissary and of

John Marret, who was one of the mutineers and since executed at Plymouth. The French commissary said they received each six louis. John Marret said they were paid each three louis and that they, the mutineers, had passports given them to go to different seaports, except Jackson, who had served in the *Pompée*, Williams, one of the men taken out of the *Bordelais*, and Ignatius Fieney, who had been an Irish priest and a lieutenant in the rebel army, which three were sent to Paris.'

'Had the mutineers of the *Danae* greater liberty when on shore in France than the men attached to their officers and their country?'

'They had and availed themselves of it repeatedly to insult their officers, who were confined in a small yard while the mutineers had about a square mile to range in. A few days after we landed, the mutineers went away from Pontanezen and the officers were then permitted the same range as had before been given to the mutineers.'

Answering the court, Niven said that McDonald had influence over the mutineers because his orders were obeyed.

'Did you see the prisoner after he was on shore and if so in what manner did he behave to you?'

Niven then told how McDonald had accused him over the pay due when Niven took him out of the transport. The first lieutenant added: 'He also came frequently to the doors of the enclosure in which Lord Proby and the officers were confined and insulted us. The particular words I do not recollect but the last time of his doing so his manner was such that I applied to the French commissary to say if he did not protect us from the insults of the mutineers we should protect ourselves. The commissary's answer was that we, the officers, must keep within the walls, and that we should be safe there.'

Then the court reached the events of only a few days before. They asked Niven: 'When you apprehended the prisoner in London, did any particular conversation pass between you?'

'He told me in answer to my asking him who were the ringleaders of the mutiny, that Jackson and James Gilliland were the first proposers of the mutiny, that it was all Lord Proby's fault, and that if his life was taken it would be the life of an innocent man; that his name was Samuel Higgins, that he was an American and had pay due to him from the merchantman in which he had lately served.

'Upon my asking for a rope to secure his arms, he said he would go with me without, which he did.'

That ended Niven's evidence, and he was the last prosecution witness. So far the captain of the *Danae* had identified McDonald as both a seaman of that name and a mutineer from the *Danae*; on top of that had come the evidence of the frigate's first lieutenant, identifying him and describing how he had arrested him in a London street.

The court then asked McDonald for his defence, and the former topman asked for time to write it out. He was provided with pen, ink and paper and the court adjourned.

The minutes record: 'When the court re-opened, the prisoner produced a written defence and a certificate from Mr Thomas Bulkeley, resident American Consul in Lisbon.'

The deputy judge advocate, Lachlan McLean, then started to read aloud McDonald's defence.

'Honorable gentlemen,' McDonald began, 'I stand here charged with having been aiding and assisting in carrying his Britannic Majesty's late ship the *Danae* into Conquet and delivering her up to his said Majesty's enemy. It is my misfortune not to have the power of bringing before this court the more positive proof that I was at Bordeaux in France at the time of the mutiny on board the *Danae*.

'Mr Joseph Lepin, an American vendor of liquors in Bordeaux, Mr Lee, a gentleman of the same place, also an American, Mme Marsh, an American woman at whose house I lodged upwards of three months, can all bear testimony that I was in Bordeaux from the time of my arrival there in the American ship *Ostrich*, of Charleston, James Wilson master, some time in February 1800 to about the month of June following; when I entered on board a schooner vessel in the French service and was employed in her on the coasting trade between Bordeaux and San Sebastian until the time of my entering on board the American schooner *Bilboa* of Philadelphia at San Sebastian in December last, in which schooner I continued until I was seized as a prisoner in London the 3rd instant.

'I most solemnly aver,' McDonald's defence continued, 'that I was not on board the *Danae* at the time of the mutiny in that ship in March 1800, that I never saw the witness Lord Proby until this day, nor the other witness, Lieutenant Charles James Niven, until the day I was taken prisoner by him in London on suspicion of being a man named McDonald, late of the *Danae*.

'I acknowledge that I told the said Mr Niven that I had heard Jackson and Gilliland declare themselves whilst in my company at Bordeaux the principal mutineers in the *Danae*, but I deny that I ever belonged to that ship.

'The certificate which I now produce from Mr Thomas Bulkeley, the resident Consul of the United States of America at Lisbon, will prove that I am a subject and a native of the said United States.

'My father and mother are now living at Hadden, in the state of Connecticut, and in no instance have I ever taken an active part in the service of any of the belligerent powers, but always used my endeavours to procure an honest livelihood as becomes a good man.'

McDonald, in his stirring declaration about belligerents, forgot that a few lines earlier in his defence he said he served in a French ship sailing between Bordeaux and San Sebastian, but he concluded:

'This honourable court will, I trust, seriously reflect upon the possibility of the witness being mistaken as to my person, particularly when it is considered that the mutineer McDonald is said to have belonged but a short time to the *Danae*. I hope my perilous case may be make known to the American Minister in London and that you gentlemen will not pronounce judgment on the life of an innocent man. Sammuel [sic] Higgins.'

The certificate (illustrated on page 33) produced in court was in fact a much creased Protection, a genuine one issued in December 1798 to a Samuel Higgins. It is a good example of the shortcomings of a Protection (the handwritten parts are shown here in italic).

Consulate of the United States of America in Lisbon.

I Thomas Bulkeley, consul of the United States of American in the city of Lisbon, do hereby certify that *Samuel Higgins* an American seaman aged *twenty five* years or thereabouts, of the height of *five* feet *seven* inches, *fair complexion, blue eyes, common nose, a native of the county and town of Hadden in the State of Connecticut* has this day produced to me proof in the manner directed in the Act intitled, 'An Act for Relief and Protection of an American seaman'; – and, pursuant to the said Act, I do hereby certify that the said *Samuel Higgins* is a citizen of the United States of America.

In witness whereof, I have hereunto set my hand, and affixed the consular seal of said States. Done in the office of said Consulate, in Lisbon the *twenty seventh* day of *December* one thousand seven hundred and ninety *eight*.

The Protection was, without doubt, issued to Higgins, or to a man who presented himself to Mr Bulkeley on 27 December 1798 as being Samuel Higgins, of Hadden, Connecticut. But whether or not there was a real Samuel Higgins, there was no such place as 'Hadden in the state of Connecticut'. There was a place called Haddam, but it is strange that a literate man – for McDonald's defence is well written – should be unable correctly to spell the name of his birthplace.

However, a reading of his defence and the production of Samuel Higgins's Protection had not ended the case. Mr Lachlan McLean, the deputy judge advocate, had some evidence to give.

The court told him: 'Relate to the court what passed between you and the prisoner on board the *Zealand* on Monday last.'

'I delivered the prisoner a letter from myself,' McLean said, 'acquainting him I was to act as deputy judge advocate and enclosing a copy of the charges against him, also a copy of the list of the *Danae's* ship's company. I asked him whether he had any witnesses to call upon in his defence and told him that if he had he should give their names to me. He said he had no one to call upon but himself.

'Upon my returning to the quarterdeck of the *Zealand* I understood from Captain Mitchell that the prisoner asserted he was not on board the *Danae* at the time of the mutiny. I then went down to the prisoner again and told him of the conversation I had held with Captain Mitchell and explained to him that if he meant to say he was not on board the *Danae* at the time of the mutiny, it would be necessary for him to give me the names of such persons as could prove that circumstance. And that if he could make it appear so to the court he would, of course, be acquitted.

'He appeared extremely agitated and said he had no one to call on but himself, that he was innocent and God Almighty help him, or some words to that effect. I told him that after Wednesday it would be too late to call any evidence.'

Hardly surprisingly, the court decided, in the face of the evidence of Lord Proby and Lieutenant Niven, that the prisoner was indeed John McDonald the mutineer, who had, at some time in the past, bought the Protection in the name of Higgins and in which he now tried to wrap himself.

The next thing was a letter from the Admiralty to Vice Admiral Alexander Graeme, commander-in-chief in the Medway, telling him of the sentence of the court martial and concluding:

And whereas the King, before whom the said sentence together with the minutes of the said court martial have been laid by the Earl of St Vincent KB hath thought fit to consent that the said sentence shall be carried into execution; you are therefore hereby required and directed to cause the said sentence to be carried into execution accordingly on Saturday next, the 13th inst., by causing the said John McDonald alias Samuel Higgins to be hung by the neck until he is dead at the yardarm of such one of his Majesty's ships within the limits of your command as you shall judge most proper, making known the occasion to the companies of all the ships and vessels under your command.

The letter was signed by Lord St Vincent, Captain Thomas Troubridge and a third member of the Board, Captain John Markham, son of the Archbishop of York.

## CHAPTER SEVENTEEN

# KING GEORGE'S
# MERCY

John McDonald had hardly been hanged before another ring-leader of the mutiny fell into the Admiralty's hands. Once again a formal letter was sent out, this time to Admiral Mark Milbanke, commander-in-chief at Portsmouth. The order quoted Lord Proby's letter from Pontanezen, and then said:

> And whereas John Williams, late belonging to the said ship, is now in confinement under strong suspicion of having been concerned in the said mutiny, we send you herewith Lord Proby's above-mentioned letter together with a pocket book containing several papers which were found on the person of the said John Williams, and do hereby require and direct you to assemble a court martial as soon as conveniently may be . . .

Admiral Milbanke gave orders to his second-in-command, Rear Admiral John Holloway, who appointed seven post captains to attend the trial on board the *Gladiator* on 12 September 1801. The captains included George Murray, who had been up to Denmark and fought with distinction in the Battle of Copenhagen since his last *Danae* court martial (of Marret at Plymouth within a few days of exactly a year earlier). The other captains – Francis Pickmore, James Newman, William Cracraft, Richard Dacres, Richard Retalick and Zachary Mudge – were all men high up on the post list.

Although the mutiny had taken place a year and a half earlier, the prosecution had been able to assemble a number of witnesses. Obviously the most important one was Lord Proby, still without a ship; others were Midshipman Spencer, the youngster who had fled to the galley, the former second lieutenant, the Hon. James Rollo, now serving in the *Ganges*, Samuel Perkins, the ordinary seaman who, although only twenty-four years old, had been one of the longest serving of the Danaes and, like Proby, came from Huntingdonshire, Thomas Olding, who had been the frigate's armourer, and a newcomer to the *Danae* trials, Mr Nicholas Kortwright, master of a transport.

Williams, like his fellow ringleader McDonald, could only claim that coincidence could be a killer, as the evidence produced before the court, along with the pocket book, soon made clear.

The first witness was, as usual, Lord Proby, who identified Williams as one of the *Danae*'s quarter-gunners. Then the court told Proby to describe what happened during the mutiny.

'The night was so dark as no person could be distinguished at the first but by their voices,' he stated. 'I heard the prisoner's voice frequently cheering and calling for a good lookout forward.

'When it was daylight the officers could see occasionally up one of the hatchways and Williams was more than once observed, consulting among those who were understood to be the ringleaders.

'When we were landed in France Williams went with the party who declared themselves disloyal. When the officers observed him consulting with the ringleaders he was armed as the other mutineers were, with a brace of pistols in his belt.'

When Lord Proby was removed from the *Danae* by the French troops, the court asked, did any of the men 'attach themselves to your Lordship to prove the loyalty they had to their King and country?'

He replied: 'Most of those who were below during the mutiny remained as prisoners of war together with myself and the other officers.'

In answer to another question, Proby said: 'Some days after we were landed I understand that one or two would have given themselves up and returned to England with me on condition of pardon, which I could not grant, but I never heard that the prisoner made any overture of the kind.'

'At what time did the mutiny take place?'

'It was about nine o'clock. I was going to bed and the Marine officer ran in to report that there was some disturbance upon deck.

Scarcely a moment passed between that and my being wounded in attempting to go up on deck and when I recovered my senses the first lieutenant reported that the hatches were all laid down and secured.'

'Did your Lordship make any attempt after that to get upon deck?' the court inquired.

'The hatches were so strongly secured that any attempt even if we had a sufficiency of arms would have been fruitless, and of course I could only make such dispositions as I thought best to force the mutineers to open the hatches and come down to us.'

'Did the prisoner, when you saw him with the pistols in his girdle, attempt to suppress the mutiny?'

'I never heard nor saw the most distant inclination in the prisoner to do anything but assist the mutineers and I have always considered him as a principal ringleader.'

The court, having finished its questioning of Proby, then asked Williams if he had anything to ask him.

'Do you recollect a question being asked from the deck,' Williams said, 'whether it would be accepted from those who remained neutral to come down to you, and it was answered no, as you considered them to be the same as the mutineers?'

'I do not recollect any offer being made of the kind,' Proby answered, 'nor do I believe the officers would have answered it without consulting me. But if it had been made, I must have answered that I thought the neutrals even worse than the active mutineers. The mutineers were offered officially from me by the first lieutenant, the surgeon, and the chaplain, by the latter twice, that if they would give the ship up I was ready to go immediately to Plymouth and transmit to the Admiralty any complaint they might have to make of the officers' conduct.'

The next prosecution witness was Midshipman William Spencer, who was sworn and then identified Williams.

'Where were you on the morning after the mutiny happened?' the court asked.

'Upon deck.'

He did not see Williams 'aiding and assisting in working the ship', he said, and was himself on deck when the mutiny broke out.

'Were you kept upon deck by the mutineers, or did you stay there of your own choice?'

'I stayed there of my own choice because I did not know where I was safest.'

The midshipman was later asked: 'Do you recollect any of the mutineers who hailed one of the forts when the *Danae* was going into Conquet?'

'Yes.'

'Did the prisoner hail the fort?'

'Yes,' said Spencer, probably overwhelmed by his surroundings.

'Relate to the court what he said at the time he hailed the fort.'

'To the best of my understanding as he spoke French, which I understood a little, he desired the French to send a party of troops on board.'

'Did he hail the fort with a trumpet or in what manner?'

'No, he put his hands to his mouth.'

'Did you see him wave his hat to the people of the fort at that time?'

'No,' Spencer replied.

'Did any troops come on board soon after he had hailed the fort?'

'Yes, French troops who took possession of the ship.'

The court's last question before handing the witness over to Williams was: 'Did you see the prisoner in the galley?'

'I do not recollect I did,' said Spencer, but Williams immediately asked him: 'Do you recollect the ship's cook was there with you?'

'Yes.'

'Do you remember you was crying at the time?'

'Yes.'

'Did you hear fresh questions asked another young gentleman there with you?'

'No.'

'Had I been disabled in my foot about two days before by a 6-pounder jamming?'

'Yes.'

'Do you recollect I was not able to get on deck at the time of the mutiny only as I took hold of things to get along?'

'He sometimes put his foot upon deck,' Spencer explained to the court, 'sometimes not, resting his foot occasionally.'

The next witness was the *Danae's* former second lieutenant, James Rollo, who had come over from the *Ganges* to give evidence.

He was just going to bed when the mutiny happened, he told the court. 'I heard a confused noise on deck and immediately afterwards the Marine officer called out that the people had mutinied.

'I immediately went to my cabin and brought out a brace of pistols, gave one to the surgeon who was still up. We, both armed, went to the after hatchway but found it battened down. We returned to the cabin, where we saw Lord Proby and the rest of the officers. Lord Proby's head was bleeding very much. He consulted us if there were any means of getting on deck.'

Asked by the court if there were any lights below to distinguish who was there, Rollo said there were, but he did not see Williams. However, he said, when he went off in the French boat he saw Williams 'sitting on the hammock cloth just by the after hatchway. He was looking over.'

Did Rollo see anything of Williams after being landed in France? the court asked.

'He was in the same prison but had the liberty of walking about the prison, which was very large.'

'When you were removed from that prison in order to come to England, what became of the prisoner?'

'We understood he went to Paris. He did not come with us.'

When it was Williams's turn to question Lieutenant Rollo, he asked: 'Do you recollect two days before the ship was carried in that I hurt my leg and was disabled from getting about?'

'Yes, I do.'

'Was he on the sick list?' the court asked.

'Yes.'

The next prosecution witness was Samuel Perkins, an ordinary seaman who told the court he was in his berth opposite the main hatchway when the mutiny occurred. He also said that he remembered the hammocks being cut down, and if the prisoner had been below decks at the time he would have seen him.

He also said he heard someone hail the fort at Le Conquet, and that French troops came on board soon after.

'Are you well acquainted with the prisoner's voice?'

'I was at the time,' Perkins said.

The *Danae*'s former armourer, Thomas Olding, was the next witness. He explained that he too had been in his hammock when the mutiny started; and told how the men below were mustered on Lord Proby's orders.

'When you were taken to prison in France,' the court asked, 'did you see anything of the prisoner there?'

'Yes, he was walking in the field before the prison with John Finley.'

'Do you know why the prisoner was allowed the indulgence of walking at large when you was not?'

'He remained in the ship to carry her to Brest and we were put on the shore at the fort and marched to Brest and went to prison.'

'Do you know any reason why he was at large?'

'For taking the ship into France.'

'Had you any conversation with the prisoner after you were in prison?'

'He came to the gate with a petticoat belonging to my wife and said he was sorry for what had happened and wished me well,' Olding said, but neither he nor the court elaborated on what his wife's petticoat was doing at Pontanezen.

Williams asked Olding: 'Was I sent out of a ship on board the *Danae* as a prisoner of war?'

'You came out of the *Révolutionnaire*, British frigate, but whether as a prisoner of war or not I cannot say.'

The court asked: 'When he came from the *Révolutionnaire* to the *Danae* was he put on a watch?'

It was a question designed to get the question of Williams's status as a possible prisoner of war answered, because no prisoner of war would be put in a watch.

'I cannot say if he was immediately, but he was afterwards.'

'Did he do his duty as one of the crew of the *Danae*?'

'Yes, as a quarter gunner.'

'Do you recollect the ship putting into port after he came from the *Révolutionnaire*?'

'Into Jersey, several times.'

'Was the prisoner ever confined when the ship put into port?'

'No,' Olding said.

The next witness to be called gave his name as Nicholas Kortright, master of a transport, and after taking the oath identified Williams.

'Where did you apprehend him?' the court asked.

'On board the *Statira*, an American ship in Jersey.'

'When you apprehended him as a mutineer of the *Danae* did he deny himself or confess his having belonged to that ship?'

'He told me that he was a prisoner of war on board her at the time of the mutiny.'

'Did you examine him or the master upon his report of his being a prisoner of war?'

'I did not examine him, but told him it would be well for him if that was true.

'It was on the morning of the 8th or 9th of August a lad came alongside of my vessel and said the commanding officer of the fort wished to speak to me. On my going into the fort he gave me a note saying there was one of the mutineers of the *Danae* on board the *Statira* and that Mr Shanks, the mate, was the informer.

'At which I requested the commanding officer to send a guard on the quay as the vessel was lying alongside it, saying "I will go on board myself and take the man."

'On going out of the fort,' Kortright said, 'I met the mate of the ship, who informed me that the prisoner had a pocketbook with papers in it sufficient to prove him to be one of the Danaes.

'I went on board the ship. The guard came down on the quay. I then went below after the man, who informed me he was on board his own ship and would not go on shore for me.

'I told him if he would not go by fair means I must take him by foul. I then went on deck, hailed my own vessel, and desired them to send about four stout hands. During the boat's coming the prisoner stowed himself away amongst the cargo.

'I demanded the keys of the hatches from the mate and said I would not leave the ship till I found him, as I would take every cask and bale out. On which one of the people asked if he should go and desire him to come up. I answered him yes. He went down and in a few minutes the prisoner came on deck.

'I put my hands in his jacket pockets, found nothing there but thought I felt a pocket book inside. On going to feel in his inside pockets he became obstreperous. I desired two of the people to lay hold of him, which they did, but before I could get the pocket book out of his pocket he by some means got his hand in his pocket himself, took the pocket book out and flung it from [himself] as with an intent to throw it overboard.

'It struck the starboard rigging of the ship and it flew back upon deck. The prisoner called out to one of the people, "Take care of my pocket book." One of the people picked it up and gave it to me. I pinioned the prisoner then and took him to the fort where I confined him.

'I then overhauled the papers. They were in the French language and I got a gentleman to read them, and I went to the Prince of Bouillon [Captain Philip d'Auvergne] and he sealed them up.'

A pocket book was now produced and held up by the deputy judge advocate, who asked Kortright: 'Was that the pocket book?'

'Yes, the very pocket book.'

'Do the papers written in it appear to be those which were in [it] when you first received the book?'

Kortright examined it. 'I remember those marked numbers 1,2,4 and 6 in particular. I did not examine them all.'

A clergyman, the Reverend William Howell, was now sworn, and the court asked him: 'Have you made a written translation of the papers produced into the English language?'

The court minutes say that Howell said yes, 'and produced the written translations which were read by the judge advocate and are hereto annexed'.

Unfortunately the translations are not still annexed to the minutes so we have no way of knowing what they said, although it is reasonably certain that among them was the passport issued to Williams by *Ordonnateur* Najac.

'Are those translations true?' the court asked Howell.

'They are as literal as the idiom of the two languages would permit.'

Williams now produced a written defence, and this too is not still included in the minutes, but as soon as the judge advocate had finished reading it, Lord Proby was recalled as a witness and asked:

'When the prisoner came from the *Révolutionnaire* to the *Danae* did he come to the *Danae* as a prisoner of war or to serve in the *Danae* as one of her crew?'

'I was out of the ship at the time,' Proby answered, 'but I had left orders with the lieutenant to offer Williams and the others that were with him that they should be received as volunteers if they chose it.

'The lieutenant reported when I came on board that he had made that offer and they answered they were in the French service against their wills and that they desired nothing better than to serve the English. I spoke to them myself and told them that as they were suspicious men they would be particularly watched, but if they behaved there would be no difference made between them and the rest of the ship's company.

'They made no application to be considered as other than volunteers at that or any other time until after the mutiny.'

This questioning of Proby seems to indicate that Williams's defence was that he was an American subject serving in a French privateer at the time he was captured and pressed by the *Révolutionnaire*, and that not only was he an American but he was a prisoner of war as well.

The muster roll, which told a different story, was still in *Ordonnateur* Najac's hands in Brest.

Williams, now asked if he had any questions for Lord Proby, said: 'Do you recollect my speaking to you, saying I should be glad to speak to you, and you said, you will go forward and do your duty and if you commit a crime you would give me four dozen more than another man?'

'I do [not] recollect the prisoner making any motion to speak to me, but the latter assertion that I would punish him more severely than any other man if he behaved improperly is very likely to have been used for Captain Twysden [commanding the *Révolutionnaire*] intended to have tried Williams and those men who were with him as Englishmen serving the enemy, and of course they were doubly bound when so great a fault was passed over. They had made some assertion of their being Americans, but had not the most distant proof of its truth.'

The court then asked Proby: 'Do you recollect what length of time he was in the ship before the mutiny?'

'I do not recollect the exact time, but it was long enough to do away with any suspicion I had of him.'

The court was not convinced by Williams's defence. The contents of the pocket book and the fact that he was originally from the French privateer *Bordelais* seem to have condemned the man. The court found the charges against Williams were proved and sentenced him to death by hanging.

The sentence was passed on Williams on 12 September, and he

spent more than three weeks as a prisoner on board the *Gladiator* in Portsmouth, contemplating the noose awaiting him. However, three members of the Board of Admiralty, Lord St Vincent, Sir Philip Stephens (a former Board secretary) and Captain John Markham, wrote to Admiral Milbanke at Portsmouth on 7 October. First they related how John Williams had been tried for helping in the mutiny on board the *Danae*, and how the court, having heard the charges and Williams's defence, had sentenced him to be hanged from the yardarm of one of His Majesty's ships. After relating all the orders, charges, findings and sentence at great length, the letter then concluded:

> And whereas the King before whom the said sentence together with the minutes of the court martial has been laid by the Earl of St Vincent hath been graciously pleased to extend His mercy to the said John Williams and to signify his Royal Pleasure that he should be pardoned.
>
> You are hereby required and directed to cause his Majesty's most gracious and free pardon to be made known to the said John Williams, and to give him such admonition for his future conduct as you shall judge necessary and proper on the occasion.

It is not at all clear why Williams was pardoned when McDonald, whose case was identical, even down to serving in the French privateer *Bordelais* when she was captured by the *Révolutionnaire*, was hanged on board a ship in the Medway. There is no correspondence with Mr Rufus King, the American minister in London, nor Mr Erving, the consul, whose office was in Finsbury Square.

## CHAPTER EIGHTEEN

# A DEATH
# IN BARBADOS

*I*n France by the time that Williams was pardoned all the
mutineers had received their share of the *Danae* prize money,
and they were scattering. Those mutineers who wanted to settle
down in France as weavers and farm labourers were finding the
language a problem, but the majority of the men went to sea, the
more daring probably serving in French privateers. The men from
the Channel Islands, who spoke fluent French, had little to fear if
they were captured unless, like John Marret when he was in Mill
Prison, the prisoners were inspected by someone like Lieutenant
Niven.

Mr Cooper, the Morlaix shipowner who had bought the *Danae*,
managed to charter the ship to the French government, which
urgently needed transport ships to go to the West Indies.

Out in Haiti the black revolutionary, Toussaint L'Ouverture,
had seized control of the island, and in October 1801, which was as
soon as possible after the peace negotiations were started with
Britain, and even before the actual Treaty of Amiens was signed in
May 1802, the French began assembling the fleet at Brest under
Admiral Villaret de Joyeuse to carry an army to Santo Domingo.
The army was commanded by General Leclerc, brother-in-law of
Bonaparte, having married the First Consul's sister Pauline.

The burden of preparing the expedition to Santo Domingo fell
on *Ordonnateur* Najac's shoulders, and in the course of correspondence between him and the Minister of Marine in Paris, the
Minister commented that the price paid for chartering the *Danae*
was 'very high', but he considered that Najac had yielded to 'the
urgency of the circumstances and the impossibility of finding
another ship'.

A few days later Najac was reporting to the Minister that the squadron was preparing to sail, and that the *Danae* had stowed roundshot and shells, and the bills of lading had been prepared. 'As this chartered vessel has a captain whom I do not know,' Najac wrote, 'I have put on board an old and experienced officer who will be given instructions and all the invoices.'

Within a week Najac was writing to the Minister again:

> The departure of this squadron is as near as it can be – it depends on the wind. These days the wind blows mostly from the north-west to west-north-west.
>
> The *Danae*, which sails in the Army's retinue, will be ready tomorrow. She carries 70 tons of munitions, assorted weapons and lead shot, and medical supplies – medicines, sheets and blankets ordered by the general-in-chief [Leclerc]. I am obliged to charter a second vessel.

He repeated that 'the squadron is held up by contrary winds from the west. It waits in the Roads. There are few sick, which surprises me.'

The great disadvantage of Brest, as far as the French were concerned, was always that ships could not get out with a west wind. The Goulet de Brest runs east and west, and the prevailing wind is west. In every other respect the port was a perfect base, with a fifteen-mile approach from the Atlantic protected by shore batteries and Pointe St Mathieu providing a perfect lookout place.

Three days later Najac was again reporting to Forfait: 'The *Danae* is sent to the Roads. I have given her a safe conduct in case she meets English vessels.' This was a sensible precaution because France and Britain were in that uneasy stage between the terms of the peace having been agreed but the actual Treaty of Amiens not yet signed.

Only two days later Najac was grumbling: 'The wind always contrary.' He reported that he had removed the lieutenant commanding the *Danae* and replaced him with Lieutenant Baudin, the 'old and experienced officer' he had put on board earlier.

Finally, on 12 December 1801, Najac told Forfait: 'Departed the 23 Frimaire year X the *Danae* with the squadron.'

Mr Cooper, the shipowner from Morlaix who had bought the *Danae*, sailed in the ship, and although the squadron was supposed to be sailing direct from Brest to Santo Domingo, Cooper wanted to go to the Canary Islands, where he had some business to transact in Tenerife. The archives in Brest record that Mr Cooper 'adopted a pretext which the captain accepted and the ship was separated from the squadron'. (The pretext was the need for food supplies.)

The last mention of the *Danae* in the French archives at Brest (some of which were destroyed during the German defence of the port in the Second World War) is from Najac to Minister Forfait, answering a query about the freight rate being paid for the *Danae*.

We can assume that after the Santo Domingo expedition (which ended in failure) the *Danae* went back across the Atlantic, probably to Morlaix. She may have subsequently been wrecked; there is no record of her having been captured by the British after the war began again following the breakdown of the Treaty of Amiens.

Lord Proby had in the meantime been elected a Member of Parliament. His stepmother, the Earl of Carysfort's second wife, was one of the Temples: one brother was Thomas Grenville, who was one of the Members for Buckingham town, while Richard, Earl Temple, son of the Marquis of Buckingham, was one of the two Members for the county of Buckinghamshire. It was not surprising, then, that Proby secured one of the Buckingham town seats.

By 1803 Proby received another command, the 44-gun frigate *Amelia*, also captured from the French, and was sent out to the West Indies. The main enemy in the West Indies was disease, not the French: in the twenty-two years of the war, the Royal Navy lost 84,000 men to disease or accident and 6,500 in fighting the French.

The reason for this was both simple and scandalous. The capture of one of the West Indian spice islands – each small – was always good for some cheers in the House of Commons, and no politician, let alone government, could resist that. Far more dangerous and lethal was the fact that the Prime Minister's favourite drinking companion was the bibulous and corrupt Henry Dundas, until recently Secretary of State for War, a man almost obsessed with the importance of the West Indies and later to be disgraced for stealing public money.

So, at the behest of William Pitt and Dundas, more and more troops and ships were sent out to the West Indies, to be defeated by yellow fever, malaria and blackwater fever. Disease was egalitarian: it struck down a ship's captain as easily as a landsman. It seemed to favour the newly arrived, but before it was realized how diseases were carried (mostly by the mosquito) a ship struck by yellow fever or one of the other fevers usually lost a high proportion of its men before the disease ran its course. The Army, spending all its time on land, suffered worse. For example, fifteen officers and 288 NCOs and men of three companies of Royal Artillery sailed for the West Indies in 1793. Two years later only forty-three of them were left alive and only four officers ever returned to Britain.

Soon after he arrived out in the West Indies, reporting to the senior officer at Barbados, Commodore Sir Samuel Hood, Proby was sent off to the coast of Surinam, on the South American mainland and one of the most disease-ridden areas, well south of the Trade winds and the chain of islands forming the Windward and Leewards.

The final chapter in the story of the life of William Allan, Lord Proby, is best told by three letters written from Barbados. The first is from Lord Seaforth to Lord Grenville, who was of course the Earl of Carysfort's brother-in-law.

In a letter dated 29 October 1804, Lord Seaforth wrote:

I intrude upon your Lordship at present from my knowledge of your communication with and friendship for Lord Carysfort, and my earnest desire that he should receive the enclosed in the least abrupt manner possible. For I am sorry to inform your Lordship that it contains the melancholy news of Lord Proby's death – as upon these dreadful occasions no palliation can either soften the blow or avert its effects.

I have thought it best to state the fact to Lord Carysfort in as few words as possible, and will now relate to your Lordship a few of the attendant circumstances to be communicated when and how your Lordship shall think best.

On the morning of the 16th inst. the *Amelia* came to anchor in Carlisle Bay while I was at breakfast, and Commodore Hood being instantly with me, I immediately sent a carriage to the wharf to bring Lord Proby up to Pilgrim [House]. The carriage soon returned with one of his officers from whom we learned that the yellow fever had broke out on board the *Amelia* eight days before, that the first lieutenant, the master, the surgeon and eight men were already dead, that Lord Proby had been seized by the same disease on Sunday afternoon (the 16th fell on Tuesday) and then lay in an extremely alarming situation, and this officer brought up the enclosed note.

The surgeon of the naval hospital, a very skilful man, and the medical gentleman who attends my family and also of great eminence in his profession were instantly sent on board and Commodore Hood followed them.

I directly ordered some apartments to be prepared for Lord Proby, but my house being thought too far from the shore, the Commodore desired to receive his Lordship at his house. I was not myself able to go on board as I was that day engaged to meet the Legislature of the island. The sittings were late and soon afterwards (about seven in the afternoon) I received the sad tidings of his death.

I had his body brought on shore to Government House next morning before daylight, where it lay until afternoon when it was interred.

I need not say that every compliment that the military, naval and civil departments could pay accompanied his remains. I have only to add that no man could be more universally lamented; or I firmly believe could not be more deserving of lamentation.

He appears to have been very early aware of his fate, yet the few hours he did live were entirely devoted to the most humane care for others. Till he fell ill himself he was unremittingly attentive to his crew, and even when so bad that he could not write he sent all his youngsters on shore to be out of the way of infection . . . The youngsters were on their way to the [Navy] Agent's when they saw the pendant and ensign lowered half staff down, when one of them instantly fainted away, having only said, 'Ah, my second father is gone.'

Lady Seaforth wrote:

I told you how very much delighted I was with him in the few days he was here. He remained on a cruise until the 16th October, when on rising we all saw with great joy the *Amelia* come into the Bay.

Seaforth immediately sent the carriage to the shore to bring Lord Proby up, but alas it returned with one of his officers to report his being very ill of a dreadful fever which had broken out in his ship, and of which he had lost seven men, his surgeon and first lieutenant, over both of whom he read the funeral service.

On Saturday he was taken ill himself, and when he came to anchor could not write but dictated a note to Seaforth to beg him to get him an airy lodging on shore.

Seaforth immediately had a quiet and airy apartment prepared for him in this house, and would have gone on board, but it happened to be the day of a meeting of the legislature, which made it impossible.

The Commodore [Hood], however, went and met the doctors and saw Lord Proby, and his house being nearer to the shore and cooler than this, it was decided he should go there, but it was found quite impossible to move him, as the last fatal symptoms were fast coming on, and about six that very evening, he expired.

What I feel for poor Lord and Lady Carysfort, that loved him like her own, and for his sisters, cannot be expressed, and the little I saw of him was to me so peculiarly pleasing and affectionate that I deplored his loss most truly. He must have had a charming disposition.

Hood, who knew him intimately from his first entrance into the Navy, spoke of him in the highest terms and was greatly affected by his death, and in his ship he was, both by officers and men, bereaved in no common degree.

Though in a most suffering state, his anxiety to the last seemed to be for others; his last act was to send some young midshipmen on shore to avoid infection, and he was afraid for all who were near him. He seemed (as the surgeon's mate who sat by him told us) to be before he died, deeply engaged in prayer, and he heard him say, 'Oh God, Thou art a merciful Father . . .'

Lady Hood, writing on 12 November, said:

His death, his funeral, all gave us a shock we did not at all recover for many days, and I believe an officer never died more deeply regretted by every man in his ship, where he acted the part of a father to all. When the men were ill of the fatal fever, *he* attended them in person, and read the final service over those who died.

Sunday, the day after he was taken ill, he declined having prayers read on account of the pain in his head, but in the evening he prayed most fervently to himself and exclaimed, 'Oh Lord, forgive me all my sins.' The surgeon's mate who sat by him (for the surgeon was dead) said, 'Oh sir, you have no sins to repent of!' to which he answered, 'God is a merciful Father.'

His consideration for others was so great that to the very last he made all his attendants stand to windward of him for fear of infection, and on Sunday, having had two basins of chicken broth made him, he sent for the surgeon's mate to share them with him, as he said he was sure he had need of refreshment and there was nobody to take care of him.

The Commodore was exceptionally fond of him, and much affected by his fate . . .

Even allowing that the Seaforths and Lady Hood were doing their best to soften the blow to the Earl of Carysfort, it is impossible to escape the verdict that when he had a good ship's company, Lord Proby was a thoughtful captain.

During the whole of the time he commanded the *Danae*, he was desperately short of men, and many of those he had were the dregs of the Navy; men whose only interest was stirring up trouble and doing as little work as possible.

Ireland had long been (and remains) a problem, and whereas many Irish had served England readily, the fact is that at the time of the *Danae* affair many were pressed. The question of Americans has been discussed earlier, along with Protections, and all the known facts concerning the six men from the *Bordelais* have been related, so it is up to the reader to draw conclusions.

Some of the mutineers complained to the French authorities that Lord Proby flogged them. The fact is that none of the trio brought to trial complained of harsh treatment. Marret, for example, needed every excuse he could find, but never complained of Proby's behaviour.

The final verdict on Lord Proby must be passed on the last few days of his life. It is a brave man who deliberately exposes himself to infection on behalf of his men; it is an even braver one who tries to save others at the moment death is about to tap him on the shoulder.

The final speculation, however, must be about the eventual fate of more than forty of the *Danae*'s mutineers who were never caught. Today, descendants of men like William Jackson, Ignatius Fieney, William Moreland, James Gilliland and the three Browns are alive, some of them probably in France, and all completely unaware of the activities of their forebears.

The names will be different: one only has to look at the list of prisoners of war drawn up at Pontanezen to realize how a French official writing down an English name as he heard it pronounced produced extraordinary results. Some examples are Alexander Cambel (Campbell), Christopher Holiner (Holmes), John Wilch (Welch), James Adckrann (Cochrane) and Richard Neckler (Nicholls).

At the end of the *Danae* story, we can be sure of very few facts. John Marret and John McDonald were hanged and Williams was pardoned, and Lord Proby died of yellow fever in Carlisle Bay, Barbados. The rest that is known of a fascinating story is written in papers contained at the Public Record Office in London, and in the naval archives in Brest (labelled *Le Diable Lui-même*) and Rochefort, and at Elton Hall, and has been reproduced here.

# NOTES AND
# BIBLIOGRAPHY

*Capitaine de frégate* Marot, the *Archiviste de la Marine* at the *Préfecture Maritime* at Brest, was extremely helpful to my wife and me in delving into the *Danae* files and subsequently answering questions by correspondence, and I am very grateful to Mlle Beauschene, *Archiviste de la Marine* at Rochefort and Lorient.

Sir Richard Proby extended the hospitality of Elton Hall and allowed me to use the papers in his possession.

The map found on pages viii and ix was prepared by David Charles of the Kirkham Studios.

Crown copyright material in the Record Office is reproduced by permission of the Controller of Her Majesty's Stationery Office and material from the British Museum Library is used by permission of the British Library Board.

The following abbreviations are used: PRO (Public Record Office); Adm (Admiralty series at the PRO); BL (British Museum Library); Proby (papers at Elton Hall); Brest (documents in the *Archives de la Marine* at Brest); Rochefort (documents in the *Archives de la Marine* at Rochefort); HMC (Historical Manuscript Commission).

Chapter 1

*page*
1  Any Briton: newspapers in BL collection.
3  *Hermione* mutiny: see Dudley Pope, *The Black Ship*, London & New York 1963.
4  Slow, tedious: *Sketches of Irish Political Characters*, 1799.
5  Life on board ship: see Dudley Pope, *Life in Nelson's Navy*, London and Annapolis 1981.
7  The chance came: *Spencer Papers*, Vol. II, 27 September 1796.

## Chapter 2

10  The specifications: Brest, Article 2G2–29–281.
11  *La Vaillante* to Rochefort: Brest 3E2–298.
11  Fisher: *A History of Europe*, Fontana Library, Vol. II, p. 912.
14  The *déportés*: Brest 3E2–323.
15  *La Vaillante* drags anchor: Ibid.
15  *La Vaillante*'s log: Brest.
16  Arrives in Cayenne: Brest 3E2–323.
16  Laporte's special report: Brest, Article 2G2–29–281.
17  *La Vaillante*'s orders to sail: Rochefort 1A–125.
18  *La Vaillante* sails again: Brest 3E2–341.

## Chapter 3

21  Very soon Laporte: Rochefort, court martial report on trial of Laporte.
21–2  Evidence of Perrier and Huguenin: Ibid.
23  Miraculous rescue: C. Northcote Parkinson, *Sir Edward Pellew, Viscount Exmouth*, London 1934.

## Chapter 4

25  William James: see *The Naval History of Great Britain*, Macmillan edition, London 1902, Vol. II, pp. 258–9.
27  The *Danae* had long since: PRO Adm 36/12266.
32  The position of Americans: see also Dudley Pope, *Life in Nelson's Navy*, London & Annapolis 1981.

## Chapter 5

41  The boatswain: PRO Adm 1/2319, Capt 'P' 297.
41  Until Irons: PRO Adm 36/12266 and Brest, *Danae* muster roll (this was the last one, secured by the French).
43  Chubb to Nepean: PRO Adm 1/2319.
43  Proby's covering letter: PRO Adm 1/2319, Capt 'P' 299.
45  Admiralty appoints Davies: PRO Adm 32/12266; muster roll Brest.
46  Quin warrant: PRO Adm 1/2319, Capt 'P' 303.

## Chapter 6

48 Every necessary measure: PRO Adm 1/5353.
51 Hollowood joins: PRO Adm 36/12266 and Brest.
51 On Monday: PRO Adm 1/1273, Captain's journal, *Danae*.
52 The weather: Ibid.
53 Letter to Lord Bridport: Proby, 15 November 1799.
54 Making sail in chase: journal PRO Adm 1/1273.
55 Pressing eight men: Ibid.
57 *Ethalion* rescue: Ibid.
59 The paper: PRO Adm 1/2321, Capt 'P' 234.

## Chapter 7

60 Laporte taken ill: Rochefort 1A–126.
61 Laporte's trial: Rochefort 3/9.60.
62 Letter to Lady Charlotte: Proby.
64 Burdet's orders: PRO Adm 1/2321, Capt 'P' 325.
64 Copy of *Sophie*'s orders: Ibid.
65 Newman's orders: PRO Adm 1/2321, Capt 'P' 325, Newman to Proby, 5 February 1800.

## Chapter 8

67 Taking John McDonald: PRO Adm 1/5356.
67 *Danae*'s last muster roll: Brest.
69 *Pallas* prize crew: PRO Adm 2/808 f.289. Admiralty Secretary Out-letters, 3 March 1800.
69 *Danae* sails: Brest, interrogation of Dominique Gunay and Ignatius Fieney, 10 May 1800.
70 The five Frenchmen: Brest, List of payments, dated Bordeaux 20 *Floréal* year 9.
72 William White's testimony: PRO Adm 1/5353.

## Chapter 9

73 'When I first took command': Ibid.

Chapter 10

82 White's report to Huntingdon: Ibid.
88 Spencer crying: PRO Adm 1/5358.
90 Lieutenant Niven's version: PRO Adm 1/5356.

Chapter 11

92 Allsop's sermon: PRO Adm 1/5354.
93 The only book: the muster roll is now in the Brest archives.
94 Proby described: PRO Adm 1/5353.
95 Lieutenant Rollo spots ringleaders: PRO Adm 1/5356.
97 Najac's telegraphic report: Brest, letter 291, IE 539.
98 Najac to Commissioner of Hospitals: Brest, E 594.
98 'The port is busy': Brest IE 539.
103 Julien sent more men: Brest, report of *Capitaine de frégate* Julien, 24 *Ventôse, an* 8.
104 Najac pays 72 francs: Brest, Forfait to Najac, 24 *Germinal, an* 8.
104 Citizen Gruiloire's orders: Brest, Minister's letters, 2 *Prairial, an* 8, IE 279.

Chapter 12

107 Proby's letter: PRO Adm 1/5353.
108 Lieutenant Niven about McDonald: PRO Adm 1/5356.
109 Receiving 72 francs: Ibid.
110 Ship considered improper: Brest IE 539 folio 27.

Chapter 13

115 Mr Nicholas Greetham: PRO Adm 1/5353.
116 The first question: Ibid.
129 Court verdict: Ibid.

Chapter 14

130 Forfait's letter to Najac: Brest IE 278 folio 265.
132 Mistake over money: Brest, Forfait to Najac, Letters of Minister, IE 281.

## Chapter 15

134    Lieutenant Niven to Captain Wickey: PRO Adm 1/5354.

134    Lord Proby's journal: PRO Adm 51/1273.

136    All the witnesses: PRO Adm 1/5354.

142    The report concluded: Brest, report of J. Lafosse.

144    Proby writes to Nepean: PRO Adm 1/2321, Capt 'P' 328.

144    'I have been so negligent': PRO Adm 1/2321, Capt 'P' 328A.

145    Carysfort to Grenville: HMC Fortescue 7.

145    Thomas Grenville to brother: Ibid.

146    Proby to Lady Charlotte: Proby.

147    St Vincent had written: BL Add. 31170, St Vincent letters.

147    St Vincent's second reply: Ibid.

147    Proby to St Vincent: Ibid.

148    Proby to Lady Elizabeth: Proby.

## Chapter 16

149    Trial of John McDonald: PRO Adm 1/5356.

157    The Protection in the name of Samuel Higgins, illustrated on page 33, is in the court martial file, PRO Adm 1/5356. It is very creased, as though McDonald had been carrying it in his pocket for a long time.

158    Admiralty letter to Vice Admiral Graeme, PRO Adm 2/1120, Out-letters, f. 149–152.

## Chapter 17

159    Trial of John Williams: PRO Adm 1/5358.

166    Neither the pocket book nor the Reverend Howell's translations can now be found in the trial file.

167    The King's pardon for Williams: PRO Adm 2/1120, Out-letters, f. 458–560.

## Chapter 18

169    Preparing the expedition: Brest, IE 287, f. 88, Forfait to Najac, 17 *Nivôse, an* X.

170    'A few days later': Brest 2A 2, f. 131, 2 *Frimaire, an* X.

170    'Three days later': Brest A B 2A 2–8, f. 3.

170  Najac was grumbling: Brest A B 2A 2–8, f. 9.
170  *Danae* departs: Brest A B 2A 2–8, f. 27.
171  Mr Cooper's pretext: Brest A B 2A 2–8, f. 162.
171  The last mention: Brest A B 2A 2–9, f. 53.
172  Army losses in the West Indies: F. D. Duncan, *History of the Royal Regiment of Artillery*, London 1874.
172  Lord Seaforth's letter: Proby.
174  Lady Seaforth's letter: Ibid.
175  Lady Hood's letter: Ibid.

# INDEX

*(Ranks are those held at the time.)*

Allsop, Rev. Thomas, 37, 70, 109, 136
*Amelia*, 171–6
American citizens (see also Protections), 32–5, 48
Amiens, Treaty of, 169
Anger, Jean, 70, 104
Arondel, Jacques, 70, 104
d'Auvergne, Captain Philip, 39–41, 47, 58, 166

Barthélemy, François, 14
*Bayonnaise*, 17–18
*Belle Poule*, 8–9
Berubé, J., 131–2
*Bilboa*, 149, 155
Bligh, Captain John, 149
Bligh, Captain William, 149
Bonaparte, Napoleon, First Consul, 14, 97, 103–4, 109–10, 130
*Bordelais*, 4, 48–50, 68, 71, 74–5, 87, 89, 95, 105, 118, 127, 154, 168, 175
*Brave*, 133
Breton, Jacques le, 70, 104
Bridport, Admiral Viscount, 39–40, 50, 52–3, 58
Brown I, John, 49, 88, 127–8, 176
Brown II, James, 49, 68, 76, 88, 123–4, 127, 176
Brown III, John, 49, 68, 77, 85, 87–8, 92, 112, 124–5, 128, 131, 136, 176
Brown, Thomas, 77
Buckingham, George Temple, Marquis of, 5

Bulkeley, Thomas, 33, 155–7
Byng, Admiral the Hon. John, 115

Calder, Rear Admiral Sir Robert, 135
*Cambridge*, 135, 138–9
Carcraft, Captain William, 159
Carysfort, Elizabeth, 1st Countess of, 4
Carysfort, Elizabeth, 2nd Countess of, 4, 171
Carysfort, John Joshua Proby, 1st Earl of, 3–5, 114, 144–8, 172–5
Cayenne, 13–18, 24
Chubb, John, carpenter, 28, 43–5
Church, Captain Stephen, 115
Coburn, William, Marine, 76, 80, 88, 93–4, 116–17, 120, 138, 153
Cochet, Jean-Marie, 70, 104
Cochrane, James, A.B., 30, 79, 81, 83, 89, 123, 128, 143, 176
*Colombe*, 2, 93–5, 97, 101–3, 130, 153
Cooper *et Cie*, 110, 130–1, 169, 171
Cotes, William, A.B., 89, 125
Cotton, Rear Admiral Sir Charles, 135

Darby, Captain H., 115
Davies, Thomas, carpenter, 45, 81, 89, 91, 128
Derrie, John, midshipman, 43
Dowling, Lawrence, Marine, 87, 137–138
*Droits de l'Homme*, 19–20

Drunkenness, xv
Dundas, Henry, 171–2
Durham, Captain Philip, 134

Elliot, John, 84, 126
*Ethalion*, 57–8
*Excellent*, 55–6

Falstaff, Sir John, xiv
Fieney, Ignatius, A.B., 68, 71, 89, 101,
    103, 128, 132–3, 154, 176
Fleming, John, 80, 83, 123
Flintiff, Francis, A.B., 28, 125
Flogging, xiv, 71–2, 101, 130, 175
Flynn, Andrew, 37, 46
Forfait, Pierre-A.-L., Minister of
    Marine, 2, 17, 18, 97, 103–4, 109–
    110, 112, 130, 132, 140, 169–70
Forster, Thomas, 15

Galle, Rear Admiral Morard de, 96
Galvin, Richard, 106, 112, 124, 131
Gardner, George, 89, 120, 127–8
Giles, Samuel, clerk, 30–51, 107
Gilliland, James, A.B., 28, 105, 154,
    156, 176
*Gladiator*, 115, 129, 159, 168
Goodrough, Charles, 49, 68, 88, 94, 97,
    106, 128, 143
Gosselin, Lieutenant Corbett, 29
Graeme, Vice Admiral Alexander, 158
Graves, Captain Thomas, 115
Greetham, Nicholas, 115–18
Greig, David, O.S., 49, 68
Grenville, Thomas, 145, 171
Grenville, William Wyndham, 5, 144–
    145, 172

Hall, John, 80, 84–5, 116–17, 121,
    125–6
Harris, Joseph, 126
Harvey, Vice Admiral Sir Henry, 135
Heaton, John, 45
Hendry, Thomas, surgeon, 29, 70, 81,
    107, 137

*Hermione*, xiii, 3, 58, 74, 76, 88, 115,
    127
Herron, Archibald, midshipman, 43,
    70, 77, 79–80, 82–5, 88, 121–5
Holloway, Rear Admiral John, 115,
    159
Hollowood, John, 29, 51, 70
Holmes, Thomas, A.B., 80, 83–4, 116–
    117, 126–7
Hood, Commodore Sir Samuel, 173–5
Hood, Lady, 175
*Hope*, 16
Howell, Rev. William, 166
Huntingdon, John, 72–3, 75, 78–82,
    84, 88, 118–21

Impress Service: see Press
*Indefatigable*, 19–24
Irons, David, 41
*Irresistible*, 149

Jackson, William, A.B., joins *Danae*, 45;
    starts mutiny, 74; administers oath,
    76–7; commands ship, 87; steers
    for Le Conquet, 91–3; sails *Danae*
    to Brest, 97–8; French interroga-
    tion, 101; goes to Paris, 103–4
    Mentioned: 68, 70–1, 78, 80, 85, 87,
    105, 121, 124–5, 127–8, 132–3,
    154, 156, 176
Jarvis, Thomas, A.B., 27, 89–90, 128,
    140
Jeffereys, William, 71–2, 80–1, 86, 91,
    116–17, 121, 125–6
Jervis, Admiral Sir John, see St Vincent
Johnson, William, 28
Jones, James, 85–6, 116–17, 121, 125
Joyeuse, Admiral Villaret de, 169
Julien, *Capitaine de frégate*, 102–3, 141

King, Rufus, 168
Kortright, Nicholas, 160, 164–6

Lafosse, Jean, 140
Lewis, Israel, 29, 78

Liddel, Robert, 135
Lightoff, Charles (alias Carl Leitoff), 89, 128
*Loire*, 63, 75
*Lurcher*, 55–6

McDonald, John, A.B., joins *Danae*, 67–8; commands ship, 87–9; helps French, 94; abuses Proby, 95, 108; wears cockade, 126; captured and trial, 149–58
    Mentioned: xvi, 71, 78, 80, 84, 92, 125, 127–8, 131, 136, 176
McGuire, Barney, 30, 77, 123, 143
McLean, Lachlan, 155, 157
McNulty, William, Marine, 87
*Mahonessa*, 7
Maitland, General Thomas, 37–8
*Malouin*, 70–1, 102, 110, 131, 141
Markham, Captain John, 158, 168
Marret, John, A.B., 87, 92–5, 97, 134–143, 154, 159, 169, 175–6
Marsden, William, 41, 144
*Medway*, 47, 50
*Mignonne*, 7
Millbanke, Admiral Mark, 159, 168
Mills, Thomas, purser, 29, 31, 70, 81, 107
*Miss Polly*, 15
Mitchell, Vice Admiral Sir Andrew, 135
*Moniteur*, 2, 103
Moreau, J.-J., 96
Moreaux, Mme, 122, 142
Moreland, William, 87, 89, 92, 127, 131, 136, 176
Mudge, Captain Zachary, 159
Murphy, John, 112, 126
Murray, Captain George, 115, 135, 159

Najac, Benoît Georges, *Ordonnateur*, 2, 96–104, 109–13, 130–2, 140–3, 167, 169–70
Nepean, Evan, 31, 37, 43–4, 69
Newman, Captain James, 63, 75, 159

Nicholls, Richard, 143, 176
Niven, Lieutenant Charles, 29, 37, 70, 75, 79, 81, 84, 86, 90–2, 94, 107–8, 124–7, 134–6, 149–50, 152–6, 158, 169

Olding, Thomas, armourer, 108, 160, 163–4
Origins of Danaes, 68–9, 106
*Ostrich*, 155

*Pallas*, 63–4, 69, 75
Parker, Admiral Sir William, 115
Pellew, Captain Sir Edward, 19–24, 40
Pellew, Captain Israel, 19
Perkins, Samuel, 160, 163
Pichegru, General Charles, 14
Pickmore, Captain Francis, 115, 119
Pigot, Captain Hugh, 3
*Pique*, 138–40
*Plenty*, 69–70, 98
Press and Impress Service, xiii–xiv, 32–5
Proby, Lady Charlotte, 4, 62–3, 146, 148
Proby, Lady Elizabeth, 4, 147–8
Proby, Hon. John, 145–6
Proby, William Allan, Lord, education, 5; goes to sea, 5–6; passes for lieutenant, 6; commands *Tarleton, Peterel*, 7–9; master and commander, 8; made post, 8; commands *Danae*, 9; joins ship, 28; sent to Channel Islands, 40; captures first prize, 42; gets six Americans, 48–50; joins Lord Bridport, 53–4; action against *Pallas*, 63; *Danae*'s last voyage, 70; wounded, 83; after mutiny, 90; surrenders, 94; reports to Admiralty, 107; trial, 114–29; evidence against McDonald, 150–151; evidence against Williams, 158–61; elected M.P., 171; death, 172–5

Proby, William Allan, Lord—contd
  Mentioned: 3, 29–31, 37, 47, 54–9, 64–5, 67, 71–3, 75–7, 84, 95, 102–3, 113, 143–8, 167, 176
  Protections, xiii, 32–5, 156–7, 175

Quin, Bartholomew, 46, 57

*Railleur*, 63, 65
Republican calendar, xv
*Révolutionnaire*, 19, 24, 48–9, 51, 118, 127, 164, 166–8
Robertson, Alexander, A.B., 88–9, 128
Robinson, Alexander, 128
Rollo, Lieutenant the Hon. James, 29, 51, 70, 75, 81, 89, 95, 127, 160, 162–3
Rovers, Adolphe, 14, 17–18, 23–4
Rovers, Joseph S., 14, 17–18
Rovers, Marie Justine, 14, 17, 23–4
Rowley, Rear Admiral Bartholomew, 149
Royal Navy, strength of, xiii

*St Nicholas*, 137
St Vincent, Admiral John Jervis, 1st Earl, 6, 114, 147, 158, 168
*Sans Quartier*, 42
Scarborough, Samuel, O.S., 49, 68, 89, 105
Seaforth, Francis Mackenzie, 1st Baron, 172–3
Seaforth, Lady, 174
Searle, Captain John, 57
*Sir Thomas Pasley*, 135
*Sophie*, 63–4
Spencer, George, Earl, 114
Spencer, William, midshipman, 79, 88, 93, 159, 161–2
*Statira*, 165

Stephens, Sir Philip, 168
Stevens, Lieutenant Robert, 39, 70–1, 81, 83, 89, 124, 128
*Sylph*, 57

Taylor, George, 126
Telegraph (to Paris), 103
Temple, George: see Buckingham, Marquis of
Temple, Richard, Earl, 171
Temple, Thomas, 5
Thompson, Sir Thomas B., 135
Thornton, Captain Edward, 115
*Times, The*, 1–4
Trollope, Captain Sir Henry, 115
Troubridge, Captain Thomas, 158
Turquand, Captain W. J., 63, 65
Twysden, Captain Thomas, 167
Tyler, Captain Charles, 115

*Uranie*, 55

*Vaillante* (later *Danae*), 10–18, 20–4
Voisin, Jean, 70

Waddy, Richard, midshipman, 42, 81
*Weymouth*, 59
White, William, master-at-arms, 70–2, 74, 79, 81–2, 89, 108, 126–7
Wickey, Captain John, 134–6
Williams II, John, A.B., 49, 68, 71, 76–8, 80, 87–8, 95, 103–5, 108, 123–4, 127, 131, 154, 159–68, 176
Williams, Captain Sir Thomas, 115
Wolley, Captain Thomas, 115
Wright, Thomas, 92, 127

Yorke, Captain Joseph, 115
Young, Captain F. S., 138–9